Meet the Cocker Spaniel

Cockers are the smallest members of the sporting dog family.

The Cocker Spaniel was originally bred to hunt a European migratory bird known as the woodcock, so the breed became known as the woodcock, or "Cocker," Spaniel.

Because of the Cocker Spaniel's excellent scenting ability, the breed is often used to sniff out drugs in airports.

Cockers come in three varieties: black, ASCOB and parti-color.

The Cocker Spaniel's beautiful, silky coat requires daily brushing and professional grooming every three months.

Cockers are considered dogs of high intelligence and can be easily trained.

Cocker Spaniels are excellent swimmers. Once they have been in the water, they are likely to go in more than you would like.

Cockers can adapt easily to rural or urban life, as long as they receive their daily exercise and playtime.

The Cocker Spaniel is extremely loving and forms a tight, lifelong bond with his family.

Featuring Photographs by
WINTER CHURCHILL PHOTOGRAPHY

Howell Book House
Published by Wiley Publishing, Inc. All rights reserved
Published simultaneously in Canada

For general information about our other products and services, please contact our Customer Care Department within the United States at (800) 762-2974, outside the United States at (317) 572-3993 or fax (317) 572-4002.

Wiley also publishes its books in a variety of electronic formats. Some content that appears in print may not be available in electronic books. For more information about Wiley products, visit our web site at www.wiley.com.

The Essential Cocker Spaniel is a revised edition of *The Cocker Spaniel: An Owner's Guide to a Happy Healthy Pet*, first published in 1995.

Library of Congress Cataloging-in-Publication Data
            The essential cocker spaniel / featuring photographs by Winter
Churchill Photography.
            p.   cm.
    Includes bibliographical references and index.
    ISBN 1-58245-068-4
    1. Cocker spaniel.
    SF429.C55E87 1999   99-17756
       636.752'4—dc21   CIP
Manufactured in the United States of America
10 9 8

Series Director: Michele Matrisciani
Production Team: Carrie Allen, Clint Lahnen, Stephanie Mohler, Dennis Sheehan,
    Terri Sheehan
Book Design: Paul Costello

ARE YOU READY?!

☐ Have you prepared your home and your family for your new pet?

☐ Have you gotten the proper supplies you'll need to care for your dog?

☐ Have you found a veterinarian that you (and your dog) are comfortable with?

☐ Have you thought about how you want your dog to behave?

☐ Have you arranged your schedule to accommodate your dog's needs for exercise and attention?

No matter what stage you're at with your dog—still thinking about getting one, or he's already part of the family—this Essential guide will provide you with the practical information you need to understand and care for your canine companion. Of course you're ready—you have this book!

Cocker Spaniel

SIGHT

Cocker Spaniels can detect movement at a greater distance than we can, but they can't see as well up close. They can also see better in less light, but can't distinguish many colors.

SOUND

Cocker Spaniels, like all dogs, can hear about four times better than we can, and they can hear high-pitched sounds especially well.

SMELL

A Cocker Spaniel's nose is his greatest sensory organ. A dog's sense of smell is so great he can follow a trail that's weeks old, detect odors diluted to one-millionth the concentration we'd need to notice them and even sniff out a person under water!

TOUCH

Cocker Spaniels are social animals and love to be petted, groomed and played with.

TASTE

Cocker Spaniels have fewer taste buds than we do, so they're likelier to try anything—and usually do, which is why it's important for their owners to monitor their food intake. Dogs are omnivorous, which means they eat meat as well as vegetables.

Getting to Know Your Cocker Spaniel

There is nothing more rewarding than watching the Cocker use his nose. The ability to sniff out the faintest of scents is one of the breed's best-known qualities. Originally, Cockers were bred and used as hunting dogs, and many owners and breeders continue to prove that these dogs have not lost their hunting and tracking abilities. Aside from a keen sense of smell, Cocker Spaniels are merry little dogs that fit into every environment.

The smallest members of the sporting dog family, they possess the biggest hearts. Their happy dispositions and small size make them ideal

CHARACTERISTICS OF THE COCKER SPANIEL

- Merry
- Keen sense of smell
- Very intelligent
- Highly perceptive
- Inquisitive

Properly bred and raised Cockers are great companions for children.

house dogs. Cocker Spaniels are faithful companions and very family oriented. They thrive on human companionship and will do their utmost to please their family. Their tails never stop wagging as they strive for human companionship and attention.

THREE VARIETIES

Cocker Spaniels are divided into three varieties based on coat color—ASCOB, black and parti-color. ASCOB is the abbreviation for Any Solid Color Other than Black and includes all shades of buff, chocolate and chocolate and tan. The black variety includes the colors black and black and tan. The more common parti-color includes black and white; black, tan and white (tricolor); red and white; chocolate and white; and chocolate, tan and white (chocolate tricolor). The tan points and the red and chocolate color, along with the white in the parti-colors, are all recessive colors.

COCKER CHARACTERISTICS

Cockers are intelligent and are quick learners. Sometimes they can even be considered a little stubborn, because it can take time to undo something they have learned incorrectly. Cockers are able performers in the obedience ring and, because they are so smart, can easily be trained for hunting and tracking.

Cockers can be unusually perceptive. These dogs are utterly amazing,

This buff-colored Cocker is a member of the ASCOB variety.

This black-and-white puppy and black, tan and white puppy are considered parti-colored.

as they notice any changes around the house.

Cockers are excellent swimmers and love the water. In fact, once your dog has been in the water, he may go in more often that you would like. This is especially true with the swimming pool. Cockers have been known to dive in during inclement weather. If you do have a swimming pool, make sure your dog is always supervised while in the yard. Dogs have drowned because they couldn't get out of a pool.

A Cocker with an all-black coat is considered a variety all his own.

Cocker Spaniels are extremely intelligent and can be trained quickly and easily.

Cocker Spaniels love their toys, so it is important to choose the safest ones for them to play with.

TOYS AND OTHER OBJECTS

Toys are a wonderful way of communicating with your dog. Frequently the dog retrieves a toy and brings it back to you for more retrieves. Some Cockers are natural retrievers, while others could care less. Along that same line, there are Cockers that will always pick up socks and other miscellaneous items and carry them around. Because there's always the danger your dog could eat a sock or other small object, it is best to keep these "goodies" out of his reach and to provide him with chew toys for his enjoyment.

Small toys can be easily swallowed, so watch over and account for them. These same dogs may not give up until they "kill" the squeaky mechanism, which can be quickly ingested. Safe toys are those made of hard rubber or rope bones.

Fun toys and play sessions combined with puppy training classes will ensure that your Cocker grows up to be even-tempered, healthy and happy!

Homecoming

Before bringing home your new family member, do a little planning to help make the transition easier. The first decision to make is where the puppy will live. Will she have access to the entire house or be limited to certain rooms? A similar consideration applies to the yard. It is simpler to control a puppy's activities and to housetrain the puppy if she is confined to definite areas. If doors do not exist where needed, baby gates make satisfactory temporary barriers.

A dog crate is an excellent investment and is an invaluable aid in raising a puppy. It provides a safe, quiet place where a dog can sleep. If it's used properly, a crate helps with housetraining. However, long periods of uninterrupted stays are not recommended—especially for young puppies. Unless you have someone at home or can have someone come in a few times a day to let her out to relieve herself and socialize with her for a while, a *small*

A dog crate will provide your Cocker Spaniel with a safe place to rest or play.

family are not at home during the day, try to come home at lunchtime, let your puppy out and spend some time with her. If this isn't possible, try to get a neighbor or friend who lives close by to come spend time with the puppy. Your Cocker Spaniel thrives on human attention and guidance, and a puppy left alone most of the day will find ways to get your attention, most of them not so cute and many downright destructive.

crate is not advisable. Never lock a young puppy in a small crate for more than an hour at a time!

Make sure your Cocker will have company and companionship during the day. If the members of your

Cocker Spaniels need human companionship and shouldn't be left alone for long periods of time.

ACCESSORIES

The breeder should tell you what your puppy has been eating. Buy some of this food and have it on hand when your puppy arrives. Keep the puppy on the food and feeding schedule of the breeder, especially for the first few days. If you want to switch foods after that, introduce the new one slowly, gradually adding more and more to the old until it has been entirely replaced.

Your puppy will need a close-fitting nylon or cotton-webbed collar. This collar should be adjustable so that it can be used for the first couple of months. A properly fit collar is tight enough that it will not slip over the head, yet an adult finger fits easily under it. A puppy should never wear a choke chain or any other adult training collar.

In addition to a collar, you'll need a 4-to-6-foot-long leash. One made of nylon or cotton-webbed material is a fine and inexpensive first leash. It does not need to be more than $1/2$ inch in width. It is important to make sure that the clip is of excellent quality and cannot become unclasped on its own.

If you live in a cold climate, a sweater or jacket for excursions with your Cocker Spaniel would be appropriate. Get a somewhat larger size than you immediately need to allow for growth.

Excessive chewing can be partially resolved by providing a puppy with her own chew toys. Small-size dog biscuits are good for the teeth and also act as an amusing toy. Do

IDENTIFY YOUR DOG

It is a terrible thing to think about, but your dog could somehow, someday, get lost or stolen. For safety's sake, every dog should wear a buckle collar with an identification tag. A tag is the first thing a stranger will look for on a lost dog. Inscribe the tag with your dog's name and your name and phone number.

There are two ways to permanently identify your dog. The first is a tattoo, placed on the inside of your dog's thigh. The tattoo should be your social security number or your dog's AKC registration number. The second is a microchip, a rice-sized pellet that is inserted under the dog's skin at the base of the neck, between the shoulder blades. When a scanner is passed over the dog, it will beep, notifying the person that the dog has a chip. The scanner will then show a code, identifying the dog.

7

A properly fit collar is tight enough that it will not slip over the head, yet an adult finger fits easily under it.

PUPPY ESSENTIALS

To prepare yourself and your family for your puppy's homecoming, and to be sure your pup has what she needs, you should obtain the following:

Food and Water Bowls: One for each. We recommend stainless steel or heavy crockery—something solid but easy to clean.

Bed and/or Crate Pad: Something soft, washable and big enough for your soon-to-be-adult dog.

Crate: Make housetraining easier and provide a safe, secure den for your dog with a crate—it only looks like a cage to you!

Toys: As much fun to buy as they are for your pup to play with. Don't overwhelm your puppy with too many toys, though, especially the first few days she's home. And be sure to include something hollow you can stuff with goodies, like a Kong.

I.D. Tag: Inscribed with your name and phone number.

Collar: An adjustable buckle collar is best. Remember, your pup's going to grow fast!

Leash: Style is nice, but durability and your comfort while holding it count, too. You can't go wrong with leather for most dogs.

Grooming Supplies: The proper brushes, special shampoo, toenail clippers, a toothbrush and doggy toothpaste.

not buy chew toys composed of compressed particles, as these particles disintegrate when chewed and can get stuck in the puppy's throat. Hard rubber toys are also good for chewing, as are large rawhide bones. Avoid the smaller chewsticks, as they can splinter and choke the puppy. Anything given to a dog must be large enough that it cannot be swallowed.

The final starter items a puppy will need are a water bowl and food dish. You can select a smaller food dish for your puppy and then get a bigger one when your dog matures. Bowls are available in plastic, stainless steel and even ceramic. Stainless steel is probably the best choice, as it is practically indestructible. Nonspill dishes are available for the dog that likes to play in her water.

PUPPY-PROOFING

Outside

The single best preventive measure one can take to ensure that a dog is not lost or stolen is to provide her with a completely fenced yard. If you have a fence, it should be carefully inspected to ensure there are no holes or gaps in it.

If you do not have a fenced yard, it would be useful to provide at least an outside fenced run where the puppy could safely relieve herself. Failing that, the youngster should be walked outdoors on a lead several times a day, taking care at first that the lead is sufficiently tight around her neck so that she cannot slip out of it.

Inside

You will also need to puppy-proof your home. Curious puppies will get into everything everywhere. Even if you generally keep your Cocker Spaniel close to you or in her indoor or outdoor enclosure, there will be times when she wants to explore and you cannot watch her. Make sure your home has been puppy-proofed so you can be reasonably confident she won't do serious damage to herself or your home.

Securely stow away all household cleaners and other poisonous

HOUSEHOLD DANGERS

Curious puppies and inquisitive dogs get into trouble not because they are bad, but simply because they want to investigate the world around them. It's our job to protect our dogs from harmful substances, like the following:

In the Garage

antifreeze

garden supplies, like snail and slug bait, pesticides, fertilizers, mouse and rat poisons

In the House

cleaners, especially pine oil

perfumes, colognes, aftershaves

medications, vitamins

office and craft supplies

electric cords

chicken or turkey bones

chocolate, onions

some house and garden plants, like ivy, oleander and poinsettia

9

Chew toys can come in handy when your dog is teething, or just looking to play.

This Cocker Spaniel is free to roam her backyard thanks to a fence that encloses her.

This curious Cocker takes a peek through an unlocked drawer.

products, such as antifreeze, which, unfortunately, has a taste dogs seem to love. Keep all electrical cords out of reach, and secure electrical outlets.

Make sure you have removed poisonous plants from your house and garden. Puppies put everything into their mouths, and you need to make sure there's nothing dangerous they can get into. Inside, dangerous plants include poinsettia, ivy and philodendron. Outside, holly, hydrangea and azalea are among the plants of which your puppy should steer clear. The bulbs and root systems of daffodils, tulips and others are also poisonous.

THE ALL-IMPORTANT ROUTINE

Most puppies do best if their lives follow a schedule. They need definite and regular periods of time for playing, eating and sleeping. Puppies like to start their day early. This is a good time to take a walk or play some games of fetch. After breakfast, most are ready for a nap. Sometimes it is easier for a working person or family to stick with a regular schedule than it is for someone who is home all of the time.

Most dogs reach their peaks of activity and need the least amount of rest from 6 months to 3 years of age. As they mature, they spend increasingly longer periods of time sleeping. It is important to make an effort to ensure that a Cocker Spaniel receives sufficient exercise each day to keep her in proper weight and fitness throughout her life. Puppies need short periods of exercise, but, due to the fact that their bodies are developing, should never be exercised to excess.

This Cocker is excited to go on her walk, which is part of her daily routine.

11

To Good Health

FIRST THINGS FIRST

The Cocker Spaniel is basically a healthy breed with few medical problems. However, it is important that Cocker Spaniel owners are aware of a few disorders specific to the breed.

Cocker Spaniels have been known to have chondrodystrophic disks and disk herniations. The movement needed to perform everyday tasks, such as running up hills and jumping onto furniture, requires the spine to be flexed at extreme angles, which abnormally hardened disks do not allow.

ATRESIA OF THE PUNCTA (CLOSED TEAR DUCTS)—Cocker Spaniels are prone to closed tear ducts, which may or may not need to be opened by a veterinarian. Have the ducts checked if your dog is tearing a lot.

CHERRY EYE—This is a common ailment in Cockers, as well as other short-nosed breeds. You may notice a red, cherry-like mass in the corner of the eye. This is not a medical emergency, but you should take the dog to the veterinarian as soon as possible.

COLITIS—Colitis is an intermittent inflammation of the colon. Some Cocker bloodlines are more susceptible to this than others. The stool may be bloody or blood-tinged. Colitis could be the result of undiagnosed whipworms or stress. Sometimes it happens for no explainable reason. Frequently the dog feels fine and is willing to eat. If the condition persists or the dog is acting poorly, you should seek professional help.

CONJUNCTIVITIS—This disease is common in Cockers. The conjunctiva

is the pink tissue that lines the inner surface of the eyelids and covers the front portions of the eyeball, except the clear, transparent cornea. The conjunctiva may become reddened, swollen and damaged by irritating substances such as bacteria, foreign matter or chemicals. See your veterinarian.

DRY EYE (KERATOCONJUNCTIVITIS SICA)—Dry eye is a disease in which tear production is absent or

Despite the risk of developing back problems, Cocker Spaniels are very athletic dogs.

WHAT'S WRONG WITH MY DOG?

We've listed some common symptoms of health problems and their possible causes. If any of the following symptoms appear serious or persist for more than 24 hours, make an appointment to see your veterinarian immediately.

SYMPTOMS	POSSIBLE CAUSES
DIARRHEA	Intestinal upset, typically caused by eating something bad or overeating. Can also be a viral infection, a bad case of nerves or anxiety or a parasite infection. If you see blood in the feces, get to the vet right away.
VOMITING/RETCHING	Dogs regurgitate fairly regularly (bitches for their young), whenever something upsets their stomachs, or even out of excitement or anxiety. Often dogs eat grass, which, because it's indigestible in its pure form, irritates their stomachs and causes them to vomit. Getting a good look at *what* your dog vomited can better indicate what's causing it.
COUGHING	Obstruction in the throat; virus (kennel cough); roundworm infestation; congestive heart failure.
RUNNY NOSE	Because dogs don't catch colds like people, a runny nose is a sign of congestion or irritation.
LOSS OF APPETITE	Because most dogs are hearty and regular eaters, a loss of appetite can be your first and most accurate sign of a serious problem.
LOSS OF ENERGY (LETHARGY)	Any number of things could be slowing down your dog, from an infection to internal tumors to overexercise—even overeating.

decreased. The cornea dries out and becomes painful, and can result in loss of vision. It is a common problem in Cockers.

OTITIS EXTERNA—This is an inflammation of the external ear canal that begins at the outside opening of the ear and extends inward to the

SYMPTOMS	POSSIBLE CAUSES
STINKY BREATH	Imagine if you never brushed your teeth! Foul-smelling breath indicates plaque and tartar buildup that could possibly have caused infection. Start brushing your dog's teeth.
LIMPING	This could be caused by something as simple as a hurt or bruised pad, to something as complicated as hip dysplasia, torn ligaments or broken bones.
CONSTANT ITCHING	Probably due to fleas, mites or an allergic reaction to food or environment (your vet will need to help you determine what your dog's allergic to).
RED, INFLAMED, ITCHY SPOTS	Often referred to as "hot spots," these are particularly common on coated breeds. They're caused by a bacterial infection that gets aggravated as the dog licks and bites at the spot.
BALD SPOTS	These are the result of excessive itching or biting at the skin so that the hair follicles are damaged; excessively dry skin; mange; calluses; and even infections. You need to determine what the underlying cause is.
STINKY EARS/HEAD SHAKING	Take a look under your dog's ear flap. Do you see brown, waxy buildup? Clean the ears with something soft and a special cleaner, and don't use cotton swabs or go too deep into the ear canal.
UNUSUAL LUMPS	Could be fatty tissue, could be something serious (infection, trauma, tumor). Don't wait to find out.

eardrum. Cocker Spaniels are well known for their ear problems, which many people attribute to their long, pendulous ears.

If ears are not properly cared for, they may get so infected that surgery may be required at some time. Have your veterinarian explain proper ear

If you believe your Cocker is suffering from an ailment, do not hesitate to have him checked by your veterinarian.

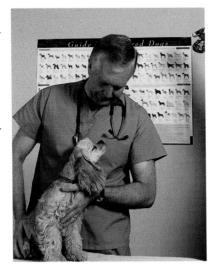

maintenance before there is a problem.

EAR MARGIN SEBORRHEA—The ear margins may have small, greasy plugs

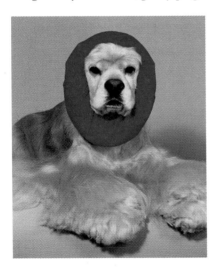

The easiest way to avoid ear infections is to use a snood wrap to prevent water from getting in your Cocker's ears while she's drinking.

adhering to the skin. This is common in some dogs with pendulous ears, and may be a permanent problem. You can remove the accumulated material with your thumbnail and wash the areas with dandruff shampoo twice a week (ask your vet which shampoo to use). Using a snood (a cloth wrap that acts like a headband to keep a dog's ears from falling into its food or water) on the dog during feeding decreases the problem.

Interdigital cysts are very common in Cockers. They are small swellings between the toes, usually associated with a staphylococcus (bacterial) infection. A home remedy is to soak the affected foot in a couple of quarts of water two times a day for two to three days. Make sure you dry the foot after the soak. If the cysts become a recurring problem, surgery may be required.

THE IMPORTANCE OF PREVENTIVE CARE

There are many aspects of preventive care with which Cocker Spaniel owners should be familiar: Vaccinations, regular vet visits and tooth care are just some.

The earlier that illness is detected in the Cocker Spaniel, the easier it is for the veterinarian to treat the problem. Owners can help ensure their dogs' health by being on the lookout for medical problems. All this requires is an eye for detail and a willingness to observe. Pay close attention to your Cocker Spaniel, how he looks, how he acts. What is normal behavior? How does his coat usually look? What are his eating and sleeping patterns? Subtle changes can indicate a problem. Keep close tabs on what is normal for your Cocker Spaniel, and if anything out of the ordinary develops, call the veterinarian.

Eyes

Cockers have beautiful eyes; therefore, it should be easy to notice anything out of the ordinary in them. Check the cornea (the clear part of the eye). Is it bright and shiny? Are the pupils of equal size? Do they constrict in response to light? Are the pupils black, or is there a gray-blue haziness or white cloudiness in them? Many old dogs have a blue haziness in their pupils, which may be a normal aging change, though you should confirm any changes with your veterinarian.

Is the third eyelid (nictitans) partially protruding over the eye? Is there discharge or evidence of tearing? Is the white of the eye (sclera) reddened or discolored? The white of the eye should never appear yellowish. Are the pink mucous membranes that surround the eye (conjunctiva) pale, normal or irritated? A conjunctivitis

Take good care of your Cocker Spaniel today and he will be healthy tomorrow.

17

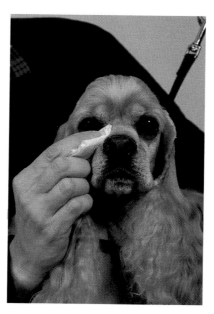

Frequently checking your Cocker's eyes will help you keep track of any changes.

or dry, dull-looking cornea could be the result of dry eye, which needs professional care.

Ears

Every Cocker owner should routinely check their dog's ears—every week for normal dogs, more frequently if there's a problem. Do the ears have an odor? Are they clean or filled with gunk? If there's gunk in them, is it wet, dry, dark, creamy or bloody?

This veterinarian is making sure the Cocker's ears are free from infection.

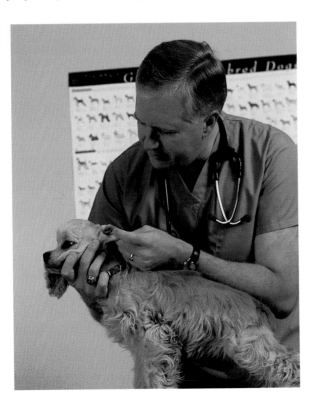

Check for swelling. Your dog can have swollen, reddened ears but no infection; regardless, this condition needs to be checked by your veterinarian. Is your dog shaking his head or scratching his ears a lot? Are the ears painful to the dog? Can your dog hear? Some older dogs lose their hearing. Unfortunately, there is no cure for deafness.

Mouth

Check your dog's mouth and get him used to your handling of it. Is there brown or yellow buildup (calculus) around the teeth? Calculus can cause the gums to recede, which results in premature loosening of the teeth (periodontal disease). Inflammation and redness around the gum (gingivitis) are usually secondary to the presence of calculus. Are there any tumors inside or outside the mouth? Check the lip folds for infection.

Skin and Coat

Is the coat shiny or dry and brittle? Are there areas of thinning hair or hair loss? Does your dog have an itching problem? Can you see skin lesions or red, inflamed areas? How about fleas and ticks: Does your dog have any of those? Is there an abnormal odor to the skin; any irritations or swellings between the toes? These are all conditions to look for and, if detected, to treat as soon as possible with veterinary assistance.

Nose

A healthy dog's nose is usually cool and moist. However, the temperature or wetness of the dog's nose is not necessarily an indication of the dog's health. A sick dog may have a warm, dry nose, or a cool, wet one. Look for other signs if you suspect a health problem.

Any secretion from the nose should be clear and watery, not thick, cloudy or colored. Most dogs have noses that are black, brown or liver-colored. There are Cockers that may have pink spots on their noses. These may or may not fill in as the dog ages. Redness or irritation could be indicative of an injury or sensitivity to sunlight. Some senior dogs have dry-looking noses.

Spaying and Neutering

Spaying or neutering—surgically altering the Cocker Spaniel so she or he cannot reproduce—should be at

ADVANTAGES OF SPAY/NEUTER

The greatest advantage of spaying (for females) or neutering (for males) your dog is that you are guaranteed your dog will not produce puppies. There are too many puppies already available for too few homes. There are other advantages as well.

Advantages of Spaying

No messy heats.

No "suitors" howling at your windows or waiting in your yard.

No risk of pyometra (disease of the uterus) and decreased incidences of mammary cancer.

Advantages of Neutering

Decreased incidences of fighting, but does not affect the dog's personality.

Decreased roaming in search of bitches in season.

Decreased incidences of many urogenital diseases.

the top of every owner's "To Do" list. Why?

First, every day thousands of puppies are born in the United States as a result of uncontrolled breeding. For every pet living in a happy home today, there are four pets on the street or in abusive homes suffering from starvation, exposure, neglect or mistreatment. In six years, a single female dog and her offspring can be the source of 67,000 new dogs.

A second reason to spay or neuter your Cocker Spaniel is to create a healthier, more well-adjusted pet that, in most cases, will live longer than

WHEN TO CALL THE VETERINARIAN

In any emergency situation, you should call your veterinarian immediately. Try to stay calm when you call, and give the vet or the assistant as much information as possible before you leave for the clinic. That way, the staff will be able to take immediate, specific action when you arrive. Emergencies include:

- Bleeding or deep wounds
- Hyperthermia (overheating)
- Shock
- Dehydration
- Abdominal pain
- Burns
- Fits
- Unconsciousness
- Broken bones
- Paralysis

Call your veterinarian if you suspect any health troubles.

an intact animal. A spayed female is no longer susceptible to pyometra (infection of uterus), and is less prone to mammary cancers. The procedure eliminates the behavior that accompanies the female's heat cycle. A neutered male is less likely to develop prostate or anal cancer and is less apt to roam. Marking behavior is also reduced by altering.

When should your Cocker Spaniel be spayed or neutered? Recommendations vary among vets, but 6 months of age is commonly suggested. Ask your vet what age is best for your Cocker Spaniel.

Vaccinations

Another priority on a Cocker Spaniel owner's list of preventive care is vaccinations. Vaccinations protect the dog against a host of infectious diseases, preventing an illness itself and the misery that accompanies it.

Vaccines should be a part of every young puppy's health care, since youngsters are so susceptible to disease. To remain effective, vaccinations must be kept current.

Good Nutrition

Dogs that receive the appropriate nutrients daily will be healthier and stronger than those that do not. The proper balance of proteins, fats, carbohydrates, vitamins, minerals and sufficient water enables the dog to remain healthy by fighting off illness.

Routine Checkups

Regular visits to the veterinary clinic should begin when your Cocker Spaniel is a young pup and continue throughout his life. Make this a habit and it will certainly contribute to your Cocker Spaniel's good health. Even if your Cocker Spaniel seems perfectly healthy, a checkup once or twice a year is in order. Even if your dog seems fine to you, he could have an ongoing problem. Your veterinarian is trained to notice subtle changes or hints of illness.

Well-Being

Aside from the dog's physical needs— a proper and safe shelter, nutritious diet, health care and regular exercise— the Cocker Spaniel needs plenty of plain, old-fashioned love. The dog is happiest when he is part of a family, enjoying the social interactions, nurturing and play. Bringing the Cocker Spaniel into the family provides him with a sense of security.

YOUR PUPPY'S VACCINES

Vaccines are given to prevent your dog from getting infectious diseases like canine distemper or rabies. Vaccines are the ultimate preventive medicine: They're given before your dog ever gets the disease so as to protect him from the disease. That's why it is necessary for your dog to be vaccinated routinely. Puppy vaccines start at 8 weeks of age for the five-in-one DHLPP vaccine and are given every three to four weeks until the puppy is 16 weeks old. Your veterinarian will put your puppy on a proper schedule and will remind you when to bring in your dog for shots.

21

Whether you're simply relaxing or running errands, your Cocker will want to be by your side.

COMMON DISEASES

Unfortunately, even with the best preventive care, the Cocker Spaniel can fall ill. Infectious diseases, which are commonly spread from dog to dog via infected urine, feces or other body secretions, can wreak havoc. Following are a few of the diseases that can affect your pet.

Rabies

Probably one of the most well-known diseases that can affect dogs, rabies can strike any warm-blooded animal (including humans)—and is fatal. The rabies virus, which is present in an affected animal's saliva, is usually spread through a bite or open wound. The signs of the disease can be subtle at first. Normally friendly pets can become irritable and withdrawn. Shy pets may become overly friendly. Eventually, the dog becomes withdrawn and avoids light, which hurts the eyes of a rabid dog. Fever, vomiting and diarrhea are common.

Once these symptoms develop, the animal will die; there is no treatment or cure.

Since rabid animals may have a tendency to be aggressive and bite,

animals suspected of having rabies should only be handled by animal control handlers or veterinarians.

Rabies is preventable with routine vaccines, and such vaccinations are required by law for domestic animals in all states in this country.

Parvovirus

Canine parvovirus is a highly contagious and devastating illness. The hardy virus is usually transmitted through contaminated feces, but it can be carried on an infected dog's feet or skin. It strikes dogs of all ages and is most serious in young puppies.

There are two main types of parvovirus. The first signs of the diarrhea-syndrome type are usually depression and lack of appetite, followed by vomiting and the characteristic bloody diarrhea. The dog appears to be in great pain, and he usually has a high fever.

The cardiac-syndrome type affects the heart muscle and is most common in young puppies. Puppies with this condition will stop nursing, whine and gasp for air. Death may occur suddenly or in a few days. Youngsters that recover can have lingering heart failure that eventually takes their life.

Veterinarians can treat dogs with parvovirus, but the outcome varies. It depends on the age of the animal and severity of the disease. Treatment may include fluid therapy, medication to stop the severe diarrhea and antibiotics to prevent or stop secondary infection.

Young puppies receive some antibody protection against the disease from their mother, but they lose it quickly and must be vaccinated to prevent the disease. In most cases, vaccinated puppies are protected against the disease.

Coronavirus

Canine coronavirus is especially devastating to young puppies, causing depression, lack of appetite, vomiting that may contain blood, and characteristically yellow-orange diarrhea. The virus is transmitted through feces, urine and saliva, and the onset of symptoms is usually rapid.

Dogs suffering from coronavirus are treated similarly to those suffering from parvovirus: fluid therapy, medication to stop diarrhea and vomiting and antibiotics if necessary.

Vaccinations are available to protect puppies and dogs against the virus and are recommended especially for those dogs in frequent contact with other dogs.

Distemper

Caused by a virus, distemper is highly contagious and is most common in unvaccinated puppies aged 3 to 8 months, but older dogs are susceptible as well. Fortunately, due to modern-day vaccines, distemper is no longer the killer it was fifty years ago.

It is especially important to vaccinate bitches before breeding to ensure maternal antibodies in the pups.

Hepatitis

Infectious canine hepatitis can affect dogs of every age, but it is most severe in puppies. It primarily affects the dog's liver, kidneys and lining of the blood vessels. Highly contagious, it is transmitted through urine, feces and saliva.

This disease has several forms. In the fatal fulminating form, the dog becomes ill very suddenly, develops bloody diarrhea and dies. In the acute form, the dog develops a fever, has bloody diarrhea, vomits blood and refuses to eat. Jaundice may be present; the whites of the dog's eyes appear yellow. Dogs with

24

though. It is only transmitted via the tick.) It is most common during the tick season in May through August.

In dogs, the disease manifests itself in sudden lameness, caused by swollen joints, similar to arthritis. The dog is weak and may run a fever. The lameness can last a few days or several months, and some dogs have recurring difficulties.

Antibiotics are very effective in treating Lyme disease, and the sooner it is diagnosed and treated, the better. A vaccine is available; ask your veterinarian if your dog would benefit from it.

a mild case are lethargic or depressed and often refuse to eat.

Infectious canine hepatitis must be diagnosed and confirmed with a blood test. Ill dogs require hospitalization. Hepatitis is preventable in dogs by keeping vaccinations current.

Lyme Disease

Lyme disease has received a lot of press recently, with its increased incidence throughout the United States. The illness, caused by the bacteria *Borrelia burgdorferi*, is carried by ticks. It is passed along when the tick bites a victim, canine or human. (The dog cannot pass the disease to people,

Kennel Cough

"Kennel cough," or the more politically correct "canine cough," shows itself as a harsh, dry cough. This contagious disease has been termed "kennel cough," much to the dismay of kennel owners, because of its often rapid spread through kennels. The cough may persist for weeks and is often followed by a bout of chronic bronchitis.

Many kennels require proof of bordatella vaccination before boarding. If your dog is in and out of kennels frequently, vaccination certainly is not a bad idea.

FIRST AID

First aid is not a substitute for professional care, though it can help save a dog's life.

Bleeding

Bleeding from a severe cut or wound must be stopped right away. There are two basic techniques—direct pressure and the tourniquet.

Try to control bleeding first by using direct pressure. Ask an assistant to hold the injured Cocker Spaniel and place several pads of sterile gauze over the wound. Press. Do not wipe the wound or apply any cleansers or ointments. Apply firm, even pressure. If blood soaks through the pad, do not remove it as this could disrupt clotting. Simply place another pad on top and continue to apply pressure.

If bleeding on a leg or the tail does not stop by applying pressure, try using a tourniquet. Use this only as a last resort. A tourniquet that is left on too long can result in limb loss.

If the dog is bleeding from his mouth or anus, or vomits or defecates blood, he may be suffering from internal injuries. Do not attempt to stop the bleeding. Call the veterinarian right away for emergency treatment.

Shock

Whenever a dog is injured or is seriously ill, the odds are good that he will go into a state of shock. A decreased supply of oxygen to the tissues usually results in unconsciousness; pale gums; weak, rapid pulse; and labored, rapid breathing. If not treated, a dog will die from shock. The conditions of the dog should continue to be treated, but the dog should be as comfortable as possible. A blanket can help keep a dog warm. A dog in shock needs immediate veterinary care.

Poisoning

A dog's curiosity will often lead him to eat or lick things he shouldn't. Unfortunately, many substances are poisonous to dogs, including household products, plants or chemicals. Owners must learn to act quickly if poisoning is suspected because the results can be deadly.

If your dog appears to be poisoned:

- Call your veterinarian and follow his or her directions.

It is important to know the first-aid basics—just in case.

- Try to identify the poison source—this is really important. Take the container or plant to the clinic.

Heatstroke

Heatstroke can be deadly and must be treated immediately to save the dog. Signs include rapid panting, darker-than-usual gums and tongue, salivating, exhaustion or vomiting. The dog's body temperature is elevated, sometimes as high as 106°F. If the dog is not treated, coma and death can follow.

If heatstroke is suspected, cool down your overheated dog as quickly as possible and call your veterinarian. Mildly affected dogs can be moved to a cooler environment, into an air-conditioned home, for example, or wrapped in moistened towels.

Insect Bites/Stings

Just like people, dogs can suffer bee stings and insect bites. Bees, wasps and yellow jackets leave a nasty, painful sting, and if your dog is stung repeatedly shock can occur.

If an insect bite is suspected, try to identify the culprit. Remove the stinger if it is a bee sting, and apply a mixture of baking soda and water to the sting. It is also a good idea to apply ice packs to reduce inflammation and ease pain. Call your veterinarian, especially if your dog seems ill or goes into shock.

INTERNAL PARASITES

Dogs are susceptible to several internal parasites. Keeping your Cocker Spaniel free of internal parasites is another important aspect of health care.

POISON ALERT

If your dog has ingested a potentially poisonous substance, waste no time. Call the National Animal Poison Control Center hot line:

(800) 548-2423 ($30 per case) or

(900) 680-0000 ($20 first five minutes; $2.95 each additional minute)

Watch for general signs of poor condition: a dull coat, weight loss, lethargy, coughing, weakness and diarrhea.

For proper diagnosis and treatment of internal parasites, consult a veterinarian.

By monitoring your pet, you will notice signs of ill health.

27

If your dog spends a lot of time outdoors, he is susceptible to bee stings, heat exhaustion and poison ivy.

Roundworms

Roundworms, or ascarids, are probably the most common worms that affect dogs. Most puppies are born with these organisms in their intestines, which is why youngsters are treated for these parasites as soon as it is safe to do so.

Animals contract roundworms by ingesting infected soil and feces. A roundworm infestation can rob vital nutrients from young puppies and cause diarrhea, vomiting and digestive upset. Roundworms can also harm a young animal's liver and lungs, so treatment is imperative.

Tapeworms

Tapeworms are commonly transmitted by fleas to dogs. Tapeworm eggs enter the body of a canine host when the animal accidentally ingests a carrier flea. The parasite settles in the intestines, where it sinks its head into the intestinal wall and feeds off material the host is digesting. The worm grows a body of egg packets, which break off periodically and are expelled from the body in the feces. Fleas then ingest the eggs from the feces and the parasite's life cycle begins all over again.

Hookworms

Hookworms are so named because they hook onto an animal's small intestine and suck the host's blood. Like roundworms, hookworms are contracted when a dog ingests contaminated soil or feces.

Hookworms can be especially devastating to dogs. They will become thin and sick; puppies can die. An affected dog will suffer from bloody diarrhea and, if the parasites migrate to the lungs, the dog may contract bronchitis or pneumonia.

Hookworms commonly strike puppies 2 to 8 weeks of age and are less common in adult dogs.

Whipworms

Known for their thread-like appearance, whipworms attach into the wall of the large intestine to feed. Thick-shelled eggs are passed in the feces and in about two to four weeks are mature and able to reinfect a host that ingests the eggs.

Mild whipworm infestation is often without signs, but as the worms grow, weight loss, bloody diarrhea and anemia follow. In areas where the soil is heavily contaminated, frequent

PREVENTIVE CARE PAYS

Using common sense, paying attention to your dog and working with your veterinarian, you can minimize health risks and problems. Use vet-recommended flea, tick and heartworm preventive medications; feed a nutritious diet appropriate for your dog's size, age and activity level; give your dog sufficient exercise and regular grooming; train and socialize your dog; keep current on your dog's shots; and enjoy all the years you have with your friend.

checks are advised to prevent severe infestation.

Heartworms

Heartworm larvae are transmitted by the ordinary mosquito, but the effects are far from ordinary. In three to four months, the larvae (microfilaria) become small worms and make their way to a vein, where they are transported to the heart, where they grow and reproduce.

At first, a dog with heartworms is free of symptoms. The signs vary, but the most common is a deep cough and shortness of breath. The dog tires easily, is weak and loses weight.

Eventually, the dog may suffer from congestive heart failure.

EXTERNAL PARASITES

FLEAS—Besides carrying tapeworm larvae, fleas bite and suck the host's

FLEAS AND TICKS

There are so many safe, effective products available now to combat fleas and ticks that—thankfully—they are less of a problem. Prevention is key, however. Ask your veterinarian about starting your puppy on a flea/tick repellent right away. With this, regular grooming and environmental controls, your dog and your home should stay pest-free. Without this attention, you risk infesting your dog and your home, and you're in for an ugly and costly battle to clear up the problem.

blood. Their bites itch and are extremely annoying to dogs, especially if the dog is hypersensitive to the bite. Fleas must be eliminated on the dog with special shampoos and dips. Fleas also infest the dog's bedding and the owner's home and yard.

TICKS—Several varieties of ticks attach themselves to dogs, where they burrow into the skin and suck blood. Ticks can be carriers of several diseases, including Lyme disease and Rocky Mountain Spotted Fever.

LICE—Lice are not common in dogs, but when they are present they cause intense irritation and itching. There are two types: biting and sucking. Biting lice feed on skin scales, and sucking lice feed on blood.

MITES—There are several types of mites that cause several kinds of mange, including sarcoptic, demodectic and cheyletiella. These microscopic mites cause intense itching and misery to the dog.

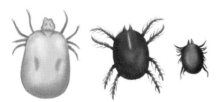

Three types of ticks (l–r): the wood tick, brown dog tick and deer tick.

Positively Nutritious

LET'S TALK NUTRITION

Anything your dog eats and digests is a source of nutrition. What your dog actually gets out of what she eats depends on the food's digestibility and how your dog's body uses the food. That's why there are good things to eat and bad things to eat. This is especially important to know if you own a Cocker, since the breed is prone to digestive upsets when their diet is changed. You should take five to seven days to wean your dog from one food to another in order to avoid gastrointestinal disorders.

There are six "building blocks" of nutrition: protein, carbohydrates, fat, vitamins, minerals and water. Each is essential to the health of your dog if well balanced.

Types of Food

There are four different types of commercial pet foods:

1. generic

2. private label

3. those marketed in grocery and feed stores (popular brands)

How to Read the Dog Food Label

With so many choices on the market, how can you be sure you are feeding the right food to your dog? The information is all there on the label—if you know what you're looking for.

Look for the nutritional claim right up top. Is the food "100 percent nutritionally complete"? If so, it's for nearly all life stages; "growth and maintenance," on the other hand, is for early development; puppy foods are marked as such, as are foods for senior dogs.

Ingredients are listed in descending order by weight. The first three or four ingredients will tell you the bulk of what the food contains. Look for the highest-quality ingredients, like meats and grains, to be among them.

The Guaranteed Analysis tells you what levels of protein, fat, fiber and moisture are in the food, in that order. While these numbers are meaningful, they won't tell you much about the quality of the food. Nutritional value is in the dry matter, not the moisture content.

In many ways, seeing is believing. If your dog has bright eyes, a shiny coat, a good appetite and a good energy level, chances are her diet's fine. Your dog's breeder and your veterinarian are good sources of advice if you're still confused.

4. those marketed in pet stores or veterinary clinics

The major differences between pet foods marketed nationally in grocery or feed stores (popular brands) and those sold exclusively in pet stores or veterinary clinics (premium brands) are: the variability and quality of ingredients used, and the emphasis on palatability versus nutrition.

Most popular pet foods are variable-formula diets. The ingredients used vary depending on their availability and cost. In contrast, many premium-brand pet foods are produced from fixed formulas, that is, the ingredients are not varied depending on cost. As previously mentioned, Cockers can be prone to gastrointestinal upsets when their food is changed. Because the ingredients in variable-formula diets tend to be inconsistent, you may decide to feed your puppy a fixed-formula diet.

There are three forms of commercially produced pet foods presently available: dry, semimoist and canned. Semimoist foods are high in sugar, are usually very palatable, have a long shelf life because of the high preservative content and produce large stool volume in the dog.

Canned foods are high in water—75 percent compared to 10 percent water in dry foods and 35 percent in semimoist foods. Canned foods are palatable but are high in sodium nitrite, which acts as a diuretic in some dogs. Both canned and semimoist foods are expensive compared to dry food. Even more importantly, they will do nothing to help your dog's teeth.

Feeding your dog a premium dry food will decrease stool volume and produce firmer stools. Dry food aids in decreasing plaque buildup on the teeth—prevention of which promotes healthier gums and teeth.

Supplements

Some pet owners believe "more is better." This can be quite harmful to your dog. Some commercial pet foods contain some nutrients in quantities that, if consumed over a prolonged period of time, may be harmful. Excessive nutrients can predispose or further the progression of diseases that affect the kidneys, heart, vascular system and skin. Urinary stones can also develop and the dog's growth can be stunted. Your veterinarian is your best source for determining the proper diet for your Cocker Spaniel.

SCHEDULE

Feeding your puppy at the same times every day in her crate will ensure that

It is important to keep your Cocker Spaniel's diet consistent so she doesn't develop any gastrointestinal disorders.

33

Feeding scraps from the table will make a beggar out of your dog in no time!

TYPES OF FOOD/TREATS

There are three types of commercially available dog food—dry, canned and semimoist—and a huge assortment of treats (lucky dogs!) to feed your dog. Which should you choose?

Dry and canned foods contain similar ingredients. The primary difference between them is their moisture content. The moisture is not just water. It's blood and broth, too, the very things that dogs adore. So while canned food is more palatable, dry food is more economical, convenient and effective in controlling tartar buildup. Most owners feed a 25 percent canned/75 percent dry diet to give their dogs the benefit of both. Just be sure your dog is getting the nutrition she needs (you and your veterinarian can determine this).

Semimoist foods have the flavor dogs love and the convenience owners want. However, they tend to contain excessive amounts of artificial colors and preservatives.

Dog treats come in every size, shape and flavor imaginable, from organic cookies shaped like postmen to beefy chew sticks. Dogs seem to love them all, so enjoy the variety. Just be sure not to overindulge your dog. Factor treats into her regular meal sizes.

your puppy will enjoy her mealtime in an undisturbed, quiet place. Give the puppy fifteen to twenty minutes to eat. After the time has elapsed, pick up the dish. If the puppy hasn't finished her food, refrain from offering her treats or other types of food. Give the puppy her next meal at the regular time. After a couple of days, you may realize you are feeding your puppy too much—adjust the portion appropriately.

The breeder will tell you how much to feed your new puppy. As your puppy grows you will need to increase the amount she is fed. Eventually, by the time she is about 6 to 8 months old, the puppy could be eating approximately 2 cups of puppy food per day.

Your puppy should be fed three times a day until about 4 to 6 months of age; generally, feeding equal portions at the morning and evening meals and a smaller portion at the noon meal. By 6 months of age, the puppy may be fed only twice a day.

Do not give milk to your puppy. After she is about 6 weeks of age, she no longer needs milk. Milk can cause diarrhea.

WATER

Clean, fresh water should be available to your dog at all times.

FEEDING THE ADULT DOG

Feed your adult dog a high-quality maintenance diet. One way to evaluate a food is by following a manufacturer's dietary program through the life stages—from puppy to adult to senior. Ask your breeder or veterinarian for a recommendation if you're not familiar with a particular food.

The average-sized adult Cocker eats approximately one and 1½ to 2 cups of a premium food daily. Of

Fresh, cool water should always be accessible to your dog.

Observing how much your growing puppy is eating will help you determine whether you are feeding her too much or too little.

FOOD ALLERGIES

If your puppy or dog seems to itch all the time for no apparent reason, she could be allergic to one or more ingredients in her food. This is not uncommon, and it's why many foods contain lamb and rice instead of beef, wheat or soy. Have your dog tested by your veterinarian, and be patient while you strive to identify and eliminate the allergens from your dog's food (or environment).

course this varies with the individual dog and her lifestyle, whether she's active or spends most of her day napping.

Whatever amount works best for your Cocker, make sure you measure it out every day. That way, if your dog gets sick and the veterinarian wants to know how much she eats, you can give a specific answer. This will help the vet enormously. Food should be served at room temperature—never too hot or too cold.

You know your Cocker's eating right when he has energy for all the things he likes to do.

WATCHING YOUR DOG'S WEIGHT

It is important that you keep an eye on your dog's weight. As most of us know, it doesn't take much to add an extra pound or two, and this could be serious for the Cocker Spaniel. A typical dog acts like she hasn't eaten for weeks. This is a sign of a normal, healthy dog.

Dogs do not need changes in their diets. If they are healthy and at normal weight, they don't get bored with their food. Avoid feeding table scraps. If you like to feed treats, take them from your dog's daily ration of food. You can measure her food, leave it on the kitchen counter or some other unreachable place, and hand out rewards from there.

Obesity is the most common nutritional disease in dogs. It can predispose your dog to heart, circulatory, liver, diabetic and pancreatic diseases. Your dog could experience heat intolerance and breathing difficulties. Cocker Spaniels are already predisposed to spinal problems; these can be exacerbated by obesity. Arthritis and torn ligaments are other problems overweight dogs suffer, simply by carrying too much weight around.

HOW MANY MEALS A DAY?

Individual dogs vary in how much they should eat to maintain a desired body weight—not too fat, but not too thin. Puppies need several meals a day, while older dogs may need only one. Determine how much food keeps your adult dog looking and feeling her best. Then decide how many meals you want to feed with that amount. Like us, most dogs love to eat, and offering two meals a day is more enjoyable for them. If you're worried about overfeeding, make sure you measure correctly and abstain from adding tidbits to the meals.

Whether you feed one or two meals, only leave your dog's food out for the amount of time it takes her to eat it—ten minutes, for example. Free-feeding (when food is available any time) and leisurely meals encourage picky eating. Don't worry if your dog doesn't finish all her dinner in the allotted time. She'll learn she should.

THE OLDER COCKER'S DIET

The older Cocker Spaniel (9 to 10 years old) will benefit from a diet of less protein and more fiber. You

GROWTH STAGE FOODS

Once upon a time, there was puppy food and there was adult dog food. Now there are foods for puppies, young adults/active dogs, less active dogs and senior citizens. What's the difference between these foods? They vary by the amounts of nutrients they provide for the dog's growth stage/activity level.

Less active dogs don't need as much protein or fat as growing, active dogs; senior dogs don't need some of the nutrients vital to puppies. By feeding a high-quality food that's appropriate for your dog's age and activity level, you're benefiting your dog and yourself. Feed too much protein to a couch potato and she'll have energy to spare, which means a few more trips around the block will be needed to burn it off. Feed an adult diet to a puppy, and risk growth and development abnormalities that could affect her for a lifetime.

can allow your older dog to keep a little more weight on than a younger dog, but never to the point of obesity. Old dogs need some reserve weight for their inevitable decline. At this time of their lives, they won't gain weight as quickly as they can lose it. Discuss this with your veterinarian.

Putting on the Dog

Grooming your Cocker can be a lot of fun, or just another chore. It can be a special time: a one-on-one situation (after all, you and your pet are best friends!)—your special time together. There are many reasons why you should keep your Cocker groomed on a regular schedule. The Cocker Spaniel is such an appealing and beautiful dog; most owners are proud to own one and want him to look his best at all times. More importantly, regular grooming allows you to physically examine your dog.

Some areas need to be trimmed short on a regular basis to prevent problems. The pertinent areas are the lip folds, around the eyes, the underside of the ears and between the pads of the feet. If hair is allowed to grow in these areas, your dog can end up with a lip fold infection, conjunctivitis and mats between the toes.

These mats can lead to sores because they're irritating, and a dog will lick at them excessively. A dog with too much hair between his toes may

Regular grooming allows you to frequently examine your dog for skin and coat problems.

even show signs of lameness. Long hair around the insides of the ears blocks off what little air is able to reach the ear canal.

SENDING YOUR COCKER TO A GROOMER

When choosing a professional groomer it may be helpful to check out how well he or she gets along with Cockers. Some don't appreciate having mats combed out. Most dogs behave very well, and yours should, too, if you acquired him from an experienced breeder who exposed your puppy to regular trimmings at an early age.

EQUIPMENT

If you intend to do any grooming at home, a grooming table is helpful, if not a requirement. Some people also use the grooming arm and noose, which are attached to the table. They, too, are helpful but not necessary. If you use the noose, do not leave your dog alone on the table. If he should jump, the noose could cause serious harm. Dogs can be easily table-trained not to jump. If a grooming table is out of your budget, then perhaps you can find some other type of table (i.e. a card table, picnic table or other small table). Whatever type of table you use, it should be sturdy.

A table used for grooming, like this one, is safe and efficient.

To groom your Cocker, you need a first-class clipper. Before choosing one, inquire about service and which clipper blades are compatible with it. Eventually, you may want two or three different sizes of blades, but for now you should start with the #10, which is the most useful.

Besides clippers, you'll need a comb (nine teeth to an inch), a pin brush to brush deep into the coat, a slicker brush, a pair of 6- or 7-inch straight shears, a pair of single-sided thinning shears and a nail trimmer. In the beginning you can get by with a clipper, nail trimmer, comb and a pair of straight shears. Combs work better than brushes for taking out mats.

GROOMING TOOLS

- pin brush
- slicker brush
- flea comb
- towel
- mat rake
- grooming glove
- scissors
- nail clippers
- tooth-cleaning equipment
- shampoo
- conditioner
- clippers

It is easiest to learn how to trim a Cocker if you are able to follow someone else's pattern. To do this, have your dog's breeder or groomer trim your Cocker, let his coat grow out for three or four weeks, then try it yourself. You will be able to see the hair that has grown out and identify what needs to be retrimmed. If you are afraid to try it, keep in mind all your mistakes will grow out and you can do better the next time.

BRUSHING TECHNIQUES

Brushing your dog is the single most important thing that you can do to

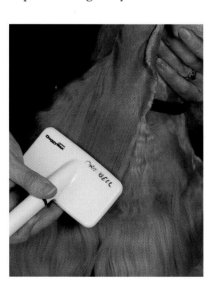

Regular grooming with a slicker brush helps prevent mats.

keep the coat looking nice and mat-free. You must brush at least every other day if you have your dog in full coat. When brushing, continually mist the hair with a conditioner spray (for example, the conditioner used as a rinse after bathing). A tiny bit of coat oil may be added to the conditioner. The conditioning mist helps avoid breaking the coat.

THE TRIM

Begin trimming with a #10 blade on the ear, starting at the flap (which is about one-third of the way down), taking the clipper against the hair up to the top of the ear and lifting the clipper a little when meeting the skull. The clipper is lifted so as not to dig into that area and create a ridge. Next hold the ear up and clip the underside, trimming very close around the opening.

At this point, start trimming the muzzle and sides of the head, paying particular attention to the lip fold areas and the corners of the eyes. These areas need to be trimmed as close as possible. Trim the whiskers and eyelashes. Long eyelashes are not proper on a sporting dog. Trim the top of the head with clippers and thinning scissors (or shears if thinning scissors are not available). Use the clippers, going with the hair, on the back half of the skull. The front half is thinned with thinning scissors, trying to give a domed appearance but not a "rooster" cut. This is impossible on some flat-skulled dogs.

Next, do the front of the neck, taking the clipper against the hair. Take the clipper, going with the hair, down the side of the neck, trying to blend it in. You would never use a clipper on the back of a show dog. The #7 blade is better, leaving the coat a little longer than the #10. Clip carefully along the back, going with the hair, and a small way down the sides. You don't want to leave your dog with a "hula skirt." Of course, if your dog is severely matted, you may not have a choice. The dog's tail can be cleaned up with thinning scissors, shears or the clipper—don't leave feathers on it.

The legs can be a challenge. Try clipping the elbow and around it with a #10 blade. This area mats easily, so it's good to clip it to prevent mats from forming. You need to comb the legs as you're working. They can be scissored short (about 2 inches) for a puppy cut, or they can be left long.

QUICK AND PAINLESS NAIL CLIPPING

This is possible if you make a habit out of handling your dog's feet and giving your dog treats when you do. When it's time to clip nails, go through the same routine, but take your clippers and snip off just the ends of the nail—clip too far down and you'll cut into the "quick," the nerve center, hurting your dog and causing the nail to bleed. Clip two nails a session while you're getting your dog used to the procedure, and you'll soon be doing all four feet quickly and easily.

43

If you can hear your Cocker's toenails click against the floor when he walks, it is probably time for a trim.

THE BATH

Make sure your Cocker is wet to the skin before gently rubbing the shampoo into his coat.

A good bathing schedule for a Cocker would be to bathe every seven to fourteen days. Follow the shampoo with a conditioner. Care should be used during the shampoo process. Excessive rubbing can cause breakage and matting. The best results will be achieved by pouring the shampoo and conditioner over the coat and gently cleansing.

Have everything necessary at hand—towels, shampoo and conditioner—ready before you put your Cocker Spaniel in the tub. Clean your dog's ears if necessary and place a small ball of cotton in the ears to soak up any water accidentally entering the ear canal (a common cause of infection). Place a rubber mat or towel on the bottom of the sink or bathtub. A hand-held rubber spray attached to your faucet can make things much easier.

Make sure your dog is completely wet before applying shampoo. Apply dabs of shampoo to the back, each leg and under the tail of your dog. Work up a good lather down to the skin, proceeding from back to front. Take special care to clean the anal area and paw pads. Rinse the coat thoroughly and shampoo again. Rinse again.

The most important thing to remember about bathing is not to get water in the ears, which can promote ear infections. You don't need to get the top of the head or the top of the ears wet. These areas

are seldom dirty and can be cleaned satisfactorily with a face cloth. Take great care to avoid the getting shampoo in the eyes. Tip the head up to rinse.

A good grooming or conditioning shampoo purchased from your veterinarian or a pet shop will suffice to clean the average Cocker. There are many different types of shampoos available, especially for problem skins. Only your veterinarian should recommend a medicated shampoo. The different types control various problems, and you don't want to use them haphazardly—you could do damage to your dog's skin.

Last, but not least, you need to clean out the dog's ears with a drying agent and cotton balls. Squirt in a few drops of a solution made with equal amounts of 3 percent hydrogen peroxide and 70 percent alcohol, and wipe out the ears. This is very important after the bath, because you may have inadvertently gotten water into the ears.

Rinse every part of the body until all traces of soap are gone and the water runs perfectly clear.

45

that are more likely to have plaque buildup. Be sure to use toothpaste made for dogs. Toothpaste for humans contains ingredients that can upset a dog's stomach.

CLEANING TEETH

Dogs should have their teeth brushed—every day if possible. This is especially important for older dogs

GROOMING EARS

Apply ear powder to the inside of each ear, making certain the hair is thoroughly covered, especially at the base. Wait a few minutes to

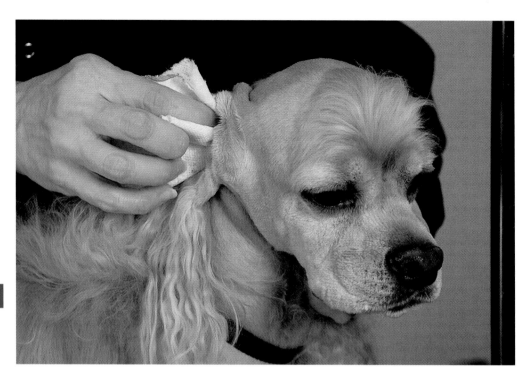

It is important to incorporate ear cleaning into your dog's grooming routine, especially after a bath.

allow the powder to dry the hair. It is surprising how much easier the hair is to pluck once the powder has dried and how much less your Cocker Spaniel will mind the plucking if the powder is used.

Pluck only a few hairs at a time, because this is less irritating for the dog. You can use your fingers to pull out the majority of the hair; however, if you prefer, you may also use tweezers or a hemostat.

Measuring Up

WHAT IS A BREED STANDARD?

All dogs come with four legs, a tail and a head with ears, eyes and a nose. So how do we differentiate a Cocker Spaniel from other dogs? We use something called a standard. This blueprint is a description that depicts the breed characteristics of a Cocker. It should, however, be remembered that the standard describes the "perfect" Cocker Spaniel. But no dog is ever perfect and no Cocker Spaniel will possess every quality in the standard.

THE STANDARD FOR THE COCKER SPANIEL

Coat

People always admire the Cocker's profuse coat, but some grow to dislike it after they own one. The standard penalizes excessive coat. The

The Cocker Spaniel is probably best known for her beautifully chiseled head and long feathering on her ears, body and legs.

48

breeder knows how to cope with too much coat and can trim it out. The pet owner may need to be an accomplished groomer, know one or be committed to regular shave downs. Many pet owners are satisfied with regular shave downs. Shave downs can sometimes be better for the dog than letting the coat grow too long, clump up and get matted. Even so, many pet owners take superb care of their Cockers' coats and keep them long and flowing.

You may want to keep this in mind when looking at puppies. Also, you need to be aware that after spaying and neutering, the coat seems to thicken. Therefore, you may want to start out with the easiest coat possible. Frequently the pet owner acquires a truly good Cocker because he is lacking in coat and can't win in the show ring. You may be lucky enough to acquire a very sound puppy that the breeder is placing with you because his coloring does not meet the standard or the markings are not showy enough to win a prize. Parti-colors are among the hardest to breed for show because the pretty spots may be in the wrong places. The markings on a parti-color dog may make or break the dog. You may acquire a liver-nosed buff or a liver-nosed red and white parti-color. Our standard does not disqualify these dogs, but it does specify that whatever color the nose is, it should be dark.

Size

According to the standard, the ideal height at the shoulders is 14 inches for females and 15 inches for males. It is possible for pet Cockers to range in height from 13 inches to more than 17 inches. Male Cockers over $15^{1}/_{2}$ inches and females over $14^{1}/_{2}$

You can get an idea of how big your puppy will grow by seeing the size of her parents.

inches will be disqualified. Males under 14½ inches and females under 13½ inches will be penalized. If you are able to see the sire and dam and perhaps other relatives, you will have a fairly good idea how big your puppy will be when he or she grows up. There is no reference to weight in the standard, but you can expect the 14-inch female to weigh approximately 18 to 22 pounds, and the 15-inch male to weigh about 24 to 28 pounds.

Bite

Many Cockers are placed in pet homes because their bites are off.

WHAT IS A BREED STANDARD?

A breed standard—a detailed description of an individual breed—is meant to portray the ideal specimen of that breed. This includes ideal structure, temperament, gait, type—all aspects of the dog. Because the standard describes an ideal specimen, it isn't based on any particular dog. It is a concept against which judges compare actual dogs and breeders strive to produce dogs. At a dog show, the dog that wins is the one that comes closest, in the judge's opinion, to the standard for its breed. Breed standards are written by the breed parent clubs, the national organizations formed to oversee the well-being of the breed. They are voted on and approved by the members of the parent clubs.

This Cocker possesses the scissors bite called for by the breed's standard.

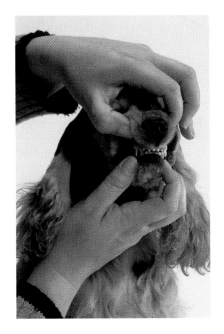

Bad bites are often the result of retained deciduous ("baby") teeth that should have been pulled. The standard calls for a scissors bite. When the bite is very undershot, the muzzle may not be as pretty.

Attitude

The standard says the Cocker should be "equable in temperament with no suggestion of timidity. Above all, he must be free, merry, sound, well balanced throughout, and in action show a keen inclination to work." Unfortunately, there are many Cockers that

don't live up to the breeder's high expectations, or meet the standard. If puppies don't receive proper training and socialization this may deter them from reaching their full potential as show dogs, breeding stock and perhaps from functioning as well-adjusted pets.

Do not pass up a good dog with a minor fault that has all the other qualities you desire.

REVISED STANDARD FOR THE COCKER SPANIEL

The Board of Directors of the American Kennel Club has approved the following revised Standard for the Cocker Spaniel as submitted by the American Spaniel Club, Inc.:

General Appearance

The Cocker Spaniel has a sturdy, compact body and a cleanly chiseled and refined head, with the overall dog in complete balance and of ideal size. He stands well up at the shoulder on straight forelegs with a topline sloping slightly toward strong, moderately bent, muscular quarters. He is a dog capable of considerable speed, combined with great endurance.

These Cocker pups enjoy the company of a Collie friend.

Above all, he must be free and merry, sound, well balanced throughout and in action show a keen inclination to work. A dog well balanced in all parts is more desirable than a dog with strongly contrasting good points and faults.

Size, Proportion, Substance

SIZE—The ideal height at the withers for an adult dog is 15 inches and for an adult bitch, 14 inches. Height may vary one half inch above or below this idea. A dog whose height exceeds $15^{1}/_{2}$ inches or a bitch whose height exceeds $14^{1}/_{2}$ inches shall be disqualified. An adult dog whose height is less than $14^{1}/_{2}$ inches and

an adult bitch whose height is less than $13^{1}/_{2}$ inches shall be penalized. Height is determined by a line perpendicular to the ground from the top of the shoulder blades, the dog standing naturally with its forelegs

51

The Cocker Spaniel is the smallest member of the Sporting group.

and lower hind legs parallel to the line of measurement.

PROPORTION—The measurement from the breast bone to back of thigh is slightly longer than the measurement from the highest point of withers to the ground. The body must be of sufficient length to permit a straight and free stride; the dog never appears long and low.

Head

To attain a well-proportioned head, which must be in balance with the rest of the dog, it embodies the following:

The Cocker Spaniel's soft expression and large eyes are never to be forgotten.

EXPRESSION—The expression is intelligent, alert, soft and appealing.

EYES—Eyeballs are round and full and look directly forward. The shape of the eye rims gives a slightly almond shaped appearance; the eye is not weak or goggled. The color of the iris is dark brown and in general the darker the better.

EARS—Lobular, long, of fine leather, well feathered, and placed no higher than a line to the lower part of the eye.

SKULL—Rounded but not exaggerated with no tendency toward flatness; the eyebrows are clearly defined with a pronounced stop. The bony structure beneath the eyes is well chiseled with no prominence in the cheeks. The muzzle is broad and deep, with square even jaws. To be in correct balance, the distance from the stop to the tip of the nose is one half the distance from the stop up over the crown to the base of the skull.

NOSE—Of sufficient size to balance the muzzle and foreface, with well-developed nostrils typical of a sporting dog. It is black in color in the blacks, black and tans, and black and whites; in other colors it may be brown, liver or black, the darker the better. The color of nose harmonizes with the color of the eye rim.

LIPS—The upper lip is full and of sufficient depth to cover the lower jaw.

TEETH—Strong and sound, not too small and meet in a scissors bite.

Neck, Topline, Body

NECK—The neck is sufficiently long to allow the nose to reach the ground easily, muscular and free from pendulous "throatiness." It rises strongly from the shoulders and arches slightly as it tapers to join the head.

TOPLINE—Sloping slightly toward muscular quarters.

BODY—The chest is deep, its lowest point no higher than the elbows, its front sufficiently wide for adequate heart and lung space, yet not so wide as to interfere with the straight-forward movement of the forelegs. Ribs are deep and well sprung. Back is strong and sloping evenly and slightly downward from the shoulders to the set-on of the docked tail. The docked tail is set on and carried on

a line with the topline of the back, or slightly higher; never straight up like a terrier and never so low as to indicate timidity. When the dog is in motion the tail action is merry.

Forequarters

The shoulders are well laid back forming an angle with the upper arm of approximately 90°, which permits the dog to move his forelegs in an easy manner with forward reach. Shoulders are clean-cut and sloping without protrusion and so set that the upper points of the withers are at an angle which permits a wide spring of rib. When viewed from the side with the forelegs vertical, the elbow is directly below the highest point of the shoulder blade. Forelegs are parallel, straight, strongly boned and muscular and set close to the body well under the scapulae. The pasterns are short and strong. Dew-claws on forelegs may be removed. Feet compact, large, round and firm with horny pads; they turn neither in nor out.

Hindquarters

Hips are wide and quarters well rounded and muscular. When viewed

53

from behind, the hind legs are parallel when in motion and at rest. The hind legs are strongly boned, and muscled with moderate angulation at the stifle and powerful, clearly defined thighs. The stifle is strong and there is no slippage of it in motion or when standing. The hocks are strong and well let down. Dewclaws on hind legs may be removed.

Coat

On the head, short and fine; on the body, medium length, with enough undercoating to give protection. The ears, chest, abdomen and legs are well feathered, but not so excessively as to hide the Cocker Spaniel's true lines and movement or affect his appearance and function as a moderately coated sporting dog. The texture is most important. The coat is silky, flat or slightly wavy and of a texture which permits easy care. Excessive coat or curly or cottony textured coat shall be severely penalized. Use of electric clippers on the back coat is not desirable. Trimming to enhance the dog's true lines should be done to appear as natural as possible.

Color and Markings

BLACK VARIETY—Solid color black to include black with tan points. The black should be jet; shadings of brown or liver in the coat are not desirable. A small amount of white on the chest and/or throat is allowed; white in any other location shall disqualify.

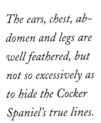

The ears, chest, abdomen and legs are well feathered, but not so excessively as to hide the Cocker Spaniel's true lines.

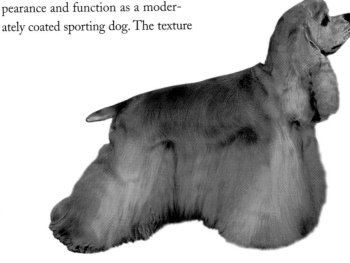

ANY SOLID COLOR OTHER THAN BLACK (ASCOB)—Any solid color other than black, ranging from the lightest cream to darkest red, including brown and brown with tan points. The color shall be of a uniform shade, but lighter color of the feathering is permissible. A small amount of white on the chest and/or throat is allowed; white in any other location shall disqualify.

PARTI-COLOR VARIETY—Two or more solid well broken colors, one of which must be white; black and white, red and white (the red may range from lightest cream to darkest red), brown and white, and roans, to include any such color combination with tan points. It is preferable that the tan markings be located in the same pattern as for the tan points in the Black and ASCOB varieties. Roans are classified as parti-colors and may be of any of the usual roaning patterns. Primary color which is 90 percent (90%) or more shall disqualify.

TAN POINTS—The color of the tan may be from the lightest cream to the darkest red and is restricted to 10 percent (10%) or less of the color of the specimen; tan markings in

THE AMERICAN KENNEL CLUB

Familiarly referred to as "the AKC," the American Kennel Club is a nonprofit organization devoted to the advancement of purebred dogs. The AKC maintains a registry of recognized breeds and adopts and enforces rules for dog events including shows, obedience trials, field trials, hunting tests, lure coursing, herding, earth-dog trials, agility and the Canine Good Citizen program. It is a club of clubs, established in 1884 and composed, today, of over 500 autonomous dog clubs throughout the United States. Each club is represented by a delegate; the delegates make up the legislative body of the AKC, voting on rules and electing directors. The American Kennel Club maintains the Stud Book, the record of every dog ever registered with the AKC, and publishes a variety of materials on purebred dogs, including a monthly magazine, books and numerous educational pamphlets. For more information, contact the AKC at the address listed in Chapter 9, "Resources."

55

excess of that amount shall disqualify. In the case of tan points in the black or ASCOB variety, the markings shall be located as follows:

1. A clear tan spot over each eye;

2. On the sides of the muzzle and on the cheeks;

DISQUALIFICATIONS

Height—Males over 15$\frac{1}{2}$ inches; females over 14$\frac{1}{2}$ inches.

Color and Markings—The aforementioned colors are the only acceptable colors or combination of colors. Any other colors or combination of colors to disqualify.

Black Variety—White markings except on chest and throat.

Any Solid Color Other than Black Variety—White markings except on chest and throat.

Parti-Color Variety—Primary color 90 percent (90%) or more.

Tan Points—1) Tan markings in excess of the percent (10%); 2) Absence of tan markings in black or ASCOB variety in any of the specified locations in an otherwise tan-pointed dog.

3. On the underside of the ears;

4. On all feet and/or legs;

5. Under the tail;

6. On the chest, optional; presence or absence shall not be penalized.

Tan markings which are not readily visible or which amount only to traces, shall be penalized. Tan on the muzzle which extends upward, over and joins shall also be penalized. The absence of tan markings in the black or ASCOB variety in any of the specified locations in any otherwise tan-pointed dog shall disqualify.

Gait

The Cocker Spaniel, thought the smallest of the sporting dogs, possesses a typical sporting dog gait. Prerequisite to good movement is balance between the front and rear assemblies. He drives with strong, powerful rear quarters and is properly constructed in the shoulders and forelegs so that he can reach forward without constriction in a full stride to counterbalance the driving force from the rear. Above all, his gait is coordinated, smooth and effortless. The dog must cover ground with his action; excessive animation should not be mistaken for proper gait.

Temperament

Equable in temperament with no suggestion of timidity.
Approved May 12, 1992
Effective June 30, 1992

A Matter of Fact

THE MAYFLOWER AND BEFORE

Would you believe that a spaniel arrived in New England after sailing on the Mayflower from Plymouth, England, in 1620? Actually, two dogs sailed; the other was a Mastiff. Although spaniels originated in Spain, they were also developed in France and England. In time, they became popular all over Europe before coming to America.

The Cocker today is derived from many types of spaniels from centuries ago. Some of these were called pet spaniels because they were small. They included the Cavalier King Charles Spaniel, the English Toy Spaniel, the black-and-white Dutch Spaniel, the red-and-white Italian Spaniel and a straight-coated, web-toed, black water spaniel called the Pyrame. Their colors are visible today in our present Cockers.

WHERE DID DOGS COME FROM?

It can be argued that dogs were right there at man's side from the beginning of time. As soon as human beings began to document their existence, the dog was among their drawings and inscriptions. Dogs were not just friends, they served a purpose: There were dogs to hunt birds, pull sleds, herd sheep, burrow after rats—even sit in laps! What your dog was originally bred to do influences the way he behaves. The American Kennel Club recognizes over 140 breeds, and there are hundreds more distinct breeds around the world. To make sense of the breeds, they are grouped according to their size or function. The AKC has seven groups:

1. Sporting
2. Working
3. Herding
4. Hounds
5. Terriers
6. Toys
7. Non Sporting

Can you name a breed from each group? Here's some help: (1) Golden Retriever; (2) Doberman Pinscher; (3) Collie; (4) Beagle; (5) Scottish Terrier; (6) Maltese; and (7) Dalmatian. All modern domestic dogs (*Canis familiaris*) are related, however different they look, and are all descended from *Canis lupus,* the gray wolf.

Originally, spaniels were bred for hunting game. They were used on land and in the water. It is said that in Spain they worked by running back and forth (quartering) in front of their master, scenting fowl such as partridge and quail, then acted as "crouchers" (setters), downing to the ground. The sportsmen would go over the field with a net, their hawks up in the air, keeping the hiding game close to the ground. The game dared not move or the hawk would get them. In those days, loading guns was time-consuming, so the hunter wanted his game to stay put; hence the net. Today, Cockers are to quarter the field, flush game and bring to hand the downed bird unharmed by their mouths—indicating a "soft mouth." In hunting tests, they also make water retrieves.

Later, spaniels were bred as sporting dogs for pleasure-seeking sportsmen, as pets for ladies and finally as show dogs. Today's Cocker is not only a woman's dog, but a man's dog, too. Even though they are the smallest dog in the AKC Sporting Group, their sturdy structure, along with their sporting instincts, make them a hardy little dog. The present Cocker is bred for show and as a companion dog, in which the dog excels. They are true family dogs.

THE 1800s

Dog showing began in England in 1859. At that time, spaniels of all varieties were shown together, but eventually they were separated into land and water spaniels. In about 1870, the Land Spaniels were re-named Field Spaniels, which included Cockers and Springers. They were then divided by weight (under 25 pounds and over 25 pounds) into two varieties—Field and Cocker Spaniels. It was possible for littermates to be registered as different varieties since size was the only criteria!

In 1891, the American Spaniel Club was formed and their first order of business was to separate Cocker Spaniels from Field Spaniels. At that time, the main differences between the two breeds were weight, height and length of body. A Cocker could weigh between 18 and 28 pounds (which is normal weight today). The Field Spaniel was to be proportionately heavier and lower and longer than the Cocker. The latter's weight limitation in the Cocker was replaced by height limits.

THE PROPER NAME

Only in this country does the name Cocker Spaniel stand for American

Cocker. Outside of this country the name Cocker refers to the English Cocker Spaniel. A few years ago the question of renaming the Cocker to the American Cocker was presented for a vote to the American Spaniel Club. It was the wish of the membership to continue with the name Cocker Spaniel.

According to English history, the red-and-whites and the black-and-whites were more common than the black Cockers. When black Cockers appeared, they were much in demand. During the early days in this country, black was supreme in registrations and popularity. Eventually attitudes regarding the colors changed and registration increased in black-and-whites, reds and red-and-whites. The red-and-whites had a hard time holding their own against the striking black-and-whites in the show ring.

The Cocker's keen sense of smell made him a great hunter and retriever.

SEPARATION OF THE AMERICAN AND ENGLISH COCKER SPANIELS

The Cocker and the English Cocker owe their heritages to a common ancestor, Ch. Obo, whelped in 1879. Ch. Obo became the founder of the English Cocker. He was bred to Ch. Chloe II, who was shipped to America. In 1882, Ch. Chloe whelped a son, Obo II, who is the progenitor of Cocker Spaniels. Ch. Obo II's conformation does not resemble our present Cockers, or at least it isn't supposed to. In his day, Ch. Obo II was a fine dog. He weighed 22 pounds, but was only 10 inches tall, and 29 inches from nose to the root of his tail.

The American Kennel Club, formed in 1884, separated the Cocker and Field Spaniels in 1905. This had already been accomplished by the English Kennel Club in 1893. Since the beginning of the AKC Stud Book in 1888, there has been no interbreeding in the United States. However, the English Cockers did not receive their own breed status until 1946, thanks to the efforts of Geraldine Rockefeller Dodge. The Cocker Spaniel and the English Cocker Spaniel grew further apart after World War I. The Cocker breeder preferred a shorter-backed, smaller variety and aimed for a more domed head with a shorter, plusher muzzle. The English Cocker is bigger; rangier, with a longer and narrower head; and is narrower in the chest. The Cocker wears more coat than the English Cocker.

The emergence of the black Cocker Spaniel came after the more common red-and-white and black-and-white varieties.

THE VARIETIES

Cocker Spaniels are divided into varieties, and at shows each Best of Variety goes on to show in the Sporting Group. Prior to 1945, the English Cocker was shown as a separate variety of Cockers. Until the 1940s there had been three varieties—solid (any solid color including black), parti-color and the English variety. During the early 1940s, the solid-color other than black Cockers earned their own variety—ASCOB. Therefore, for a short period of time there were four varieties of Cockers being shown.

Until the 1980s, the black-and-tans were moved from group to group. No variety wanted them. Black-and-tans started showing with the parti-colors, were cast off to the ASCOB variety, and finally landed where they belonged all along, in the black variety. It is difficult to understand why the black-and-tan dogs were not more readily accepted. Black-and-tans and chocolate-and-tans are very appealing and can be just as lovely as any other Cocker Spaniel. Today they have all come into their own and are readily sought after by breeders and pet owners.

This chocolate-colored Cocker Spaniel is one of the Any Solid Color Other than Black (ASCOB) variety.

61

TODAY'S COCKER

From the beginning of AKC regis-trations until the early 1930s, the Obo-type dog prevailed—low on leg, long in body, moderate in head and muzzle with feathering on the back of the legs and underside. A "new look" was created in the 1930s. The new Cocker was higher on leg (more up on leg), more compact and had a shorter muzzle. The feathering was the same as before—on the back of the legs and the underside of the body. Our present-day show Cocker began to make its appearance in the mid-1940s. This dog was an even taller, more compact animal, with an

FAMOUS OWNERS OF COCKER SPANIELS

Oprah Winfrey

Lucille Ball

Elizabeth Barrett Browning

Rafael Palmeiro

Ken Caminiti

Although their hunting instincts have been preserved, Cocker Spaniels are found more often on the sofa than in the field.

accentuated stop, higher dome, a shorter, deeper muzzle, more slope to the topline and a higher tailset. This Cocker carries a plusher coat—with feathering everywhere, including the front of the legs. Over the years the standard set forth by the American Spaniel Club has changed many times, with conformation changes in the most recent

years. It appears the "die has been cast." Even so, we see all different types of Cockers. Many of these are throwbacks to some of the older types.

As previously mentioned, the correct, present-day Cocker barely resembles Ch. Obo II, but the inherent instincts are still apparent. Given the opportunity, many of our lovely companion dogs would quickly take off on a hunt. Long ago there was more space and fewer cars. Obviously the world has changed dramatically during the last fifty or more years. It would be foolhardy to allow these little dogs the freedom to run the fields unsupervised. Our Cockers are family to us, and it isn't worth the risk of losing them or having them hit by a car. Nevertheless, a properly trained dog may be able to go out with a conscientious owner.

The Cocker has withstood the test of time and is still favored as a loving companion, as well as being a dog that is able to show off with style in the show ring. The interest in using the dog in hunting has grown over the last decade. This instinct has been carried over the centuries. The Cocker Spaniel is easily trained and enjoys performing in obedience.

On Good Behavior

by Ian Dunbar, Ph.D., MRCVS

Training is the jewel in the crown—the most important aspect of doggy husbandry. There is no more important variable influencing dog behavior and temperament than the dog's education: A well-trained, well-behaved and good-natured puppydog is always a joy to live with, but an untrained and uncivilized dog can be a perpetual nightmare. Moreover, deny the dog an education and she will not have the opportunity to fulfill her own canine potential; neither will she have the ability to communicate effectively with her human companions.

Luckily, modern psychological training methods are easy, efficient, effective and, above all, considerably dog-friendly and user-friendly. Doggy education is as simple as it is enjoy-able. But before you can have a good time play-training with your new dog, you have to learn what to do and how to do it. There is no bigger variable influencing the success of dog training than the owner's experience and expertise. Before you embark on the dog's education, you must first edu-cate yourself.

BASIC TRAINING FOR OWNERS

Ideally, basic owner training should begin well before you select your dog. Find out all you can about your cho-sen breed first, then master rudimen-tary training and handling skills. If you already have your puppydog, owner training is a dire emergency—the clock is ticking! Especially for puppies, the first few weeks at home are the most important and influen-tial days in the dog's life. The cause of most adolescent and adult problems may be traced back to the initial days the pup explores her new home. This is the time to establish the *status quo*—to teach the puppydog how you would like her to behave and so prevent other-wise predictable problems.

In addition to consulting breed-ers and breed books such as this one

(which understandably have a posi-tive breed bias), seek out as many pet owners with your breed as you can find. Good points are obvious. What you want to find out are the breed-specific problems, so you can nip them in the bud. In particular, you should talk to owners with adolescent dogs and make a list of all anticipated problems. Most important, test drive at least half a dozen adolescent and adult dogs of your breed yourself. An 8-week-old puppy is deceptively easy to handle, but she will acquire adult size, speed and strength in just four months, so you should learn now what to prepare for.

Puppy and pet dog training classes offer a convenient venue to locate pet owners and observe dogs in action. For a list of suitable trainers in your area, contact the Association of Pet Dog Trainers (see chapter 9). You may also begin your basic owner training by observing other owners in class. Watch as many classes and test drive as many dogs as possible. Select an upbeat, dog-friendly, people-friendly, fun-and-games, puppydog pet training class to learn the ropes. Also, watch training videos and read training books. You must find out what to do and how to do it *before* you have to do it.

PRINCIPLES OF TRAINING

Most people think training comprises teaching the dog to do things such as sit, speak and roll over, but even a 4-week-old pup knows how to do these things already. Instead, the first step in training involves teaching the dog human words for each dog behavior and activity and for each aspect of the dog's environment. That way you, the owner, can more easily participate in the dog's domestic education by directing her to perform specific actions appropriately, that is, at the right time, in the right place and so on. Training opens communication channels, enabling an educated dog to at least understand her owner's requests.

In addition to teaching a dog what we want her to do, it is also necessary to teach her why she should do what we ask. Indeed, 95 percent of training revolves around motivating the dog to want to do what we want. Dogs often understand what their owners want; they just don't see the point of doing it—especially when the owner's repetitively boring and seemingly

With proper training and guidance, these pups will grow up to be perfect angels.

OWNING A PARTY ANIMAL

It's a fact: The more of the world your puppy is exposed to, the more comfortable she'll be in it. Once your puppy's had her shots, start taking her everywhere with you. Encourage friendly interaction with strangers, expose her to different environments (towns, fields, beaches) and most important, enroll her in a puppy class where she'll get to play with other puppies. These simple, fun, shared activities will develop your pup into a confident socialite; reliable around other people and dogs.

senseless instructions are totally at odds with much more pressing and exciting doggy distractions. It is not so much the dog that is being stubborn or dominant; rather, it is the owner who has failed to acknowledge the dog's needs and feelings and to approach training from the dog's point of view.

This woman rewards her Cocker Spaniel with a tasty treat.

The Meaning of Instructions

The secret to successful training is learning how to use training lures to predict or prompt specific behaviors—to coax the dog to do what you want when you want. Any highly valued object (such as a treat or toy) may be used as a lure, which the dog will follow with her eyes and nose. Moving the lure in specific ways entices the dog to move her nose, head and entire body in specific ways. In fact, by learning the art of manipulating various lures, it is possible to teach the dog to assume virtually any body position and perform any action. Once you have control over the expression of the dog's behaviors and can elicit any body position or behavior at will, you can easily teach the dog to perform on request.

Tell your dog what you want her to do, use a lure to entice her to respond correctly, then profusely praise and maybe reward her once she performs the desired action. For example, verbally request "Fido, sit!" while you move a squeaky toy upwards and backwards over the dog's muzzle (lure-movement and hand signal), smile knowingly as she looks up (to follow the lure) and sits down (as a result of canine anatomical engineering), then praise her to distraction ("Gooood Fido!"). Squeak the toy, offer a training treat and give your dog and yourself a pat on the back.

Being able to elicit desired responses over and over enables the owner to reward the dog over and over. Consequently, the dog begins to think training is fun. For example, the more the dog is rewarded for sitting, the more she enjoys sitting. Eventually the dog comes to realize that, whereas most sitting is appreciated, sitting immediately upon request usually prompts especially enthusiastic praise and a slew of high-level rewards. The dog begins to sit on cue much of the time, showing that she is starting to grasp the meaning of the owner's verbal request and hand signal.

Why Comply?

Most dogs enjoy initial lure-reward training and are only too happy to comply with their owners' wishes. Unfortunately, repetitive drilling without appreciative feedback tends to diminish the dog's enthusiasm until she eventually fails to see the point of complying anymore. Moreover, as the dog approaches adolescence she becomes more easily distracted as she develops other interests. Lengthy sessions with repetitive exercises tend to bore and demotivate both parties. If it's not fun, the owner doesn't do it and neither does the dog.

Integrate training into your dog's life: The greater number of training sessions each day and the shorter they are, the more willingly compliant your dog will become. Make sure to have a short (just a few seconds) training interlude before every enjoyable canine activity. For example, ask your dog to sit to greet people, to sit before you throw her Frisbee and to sit for her supper. Really, sitting is no different from a canine "Please." Also, include numerous short training interludes during every enjoyable canine pastime, for example, when playing with the dog or when she is running in the park. In this fashion, doggy distractions may be effectively converted into rewards for training. Just as all games have rules, fun becomes training . . . and training becomes fun.

Eventually, rewards actually become unnecessary to continue motivating your dog. If trained with consideration and kindness, performing

FINDING A TRAINER

Have fun with your dog, take a training class! But don't just sign on any dotted line, find a trainer whose approach and style you like and whose students (and their dogs) are really learning. Ask to visit a class to observe a trainer in action. For the names of trainers near you, ask your veterinarian, your pet supply store, your dog-owning neighbors or call (800) PET-DOGS (the Association of Pet Dog Trainers).

the desired behaviors will become self-rewarding and, in a sense, your dog will motivate herself. Just as it is not necessary to reward a human companion during an enjoyable walk in the park, or following a game of tennis, it is hardly necessary to reward our best friend—the dog—for walking by our side or while playing fetch. Human company during enjoyable activities is reward enough for most dogs.

Even though your dog has become self-motivating, it's still good to praise and pet her a lot and offer rewards once in a while, especially for a good job well done. And if for no other reason, praising and rewarding others is good for the human heart.

Punishment

Without a doubt, lure-reward training is by far the best way to teach: Entice your dog to do what you want and then reward her for doing so. Unfortunately, a human shortcoming is to take the good for granted and to moan and groan at the bad. Specifically, the dog's many good behaviors are ignored while the owner focuses on punishing the dog for making mistakes. In extreme cases, instruction is limited to punishing mistakes made by a trainee dog, child, employee or husband, even though it has been proven punishment training is notoriously inefficient and ineffective and is decidedly unfriendly and combative. It teaches the dog that training is a drag, almost as quickly as it teaches the dog to dislike her trainer. Why treat our best friends like our worst enemies?

Punishment training is also much more laborious and time consuming. Whereas it takes only a finite amount of time to teach a dog what to chew, for example, it takes much, much longer to punish the dog for each and every mistake. Remember, there is only one right way! So why not teach that right way from the outset?!

To make matters worse, punishment training causes severe lapses in the dog's reliability. Since it is obviously impossible to punish the dog each and every time she misbehaves, the dog quickly learns to distinguish between those times when she must comply (so as to avoid impending punishment) and those times when she need not comply, because punishment is impossible. Such times include when the dog is off leash and 6 feet away, when the owner is otherwise engaged (talking to a friend, watching television, taking a shower, tending to the baby or chatting on the telephone) or when the dog is left at home alone.

Instances of misbehavior will be numerous when the owner is away, because even when the dog complied in the owner's looming presence, she did so unwillingly. The dog was forced to act against her will, rather than molding her will to want to please. Hence, when the owner is absent, not only does the dog know she need not comply, she simply does not want to. Again, the trainee is not a stubborn vindictive beast, but rather the trainer has failed to teach. Punishment training invariably creates unpredictable Jekyll and Hyde behavior.

Your Cocker will do anything to please you—teach her to lay down when you ask.

TRAINER'S TOOLS

Many training books extol the virtues of a vast array of training paraphernalia and electronic and metallic gizmos, most of which are designed for canine restraint, correction and punishment, rather than for actual facilitation of doggy education. In reality, most effective training tools are not found in stores; they come from within ourselves. In addition to a willing dog, all you really need is a functional human brain, gentle hands, a loving heart and a good attitude.

In terms of equipment, all dogs do require a quality buckle collar to sport dog tags and to attach the leash (for safety and to comply with local leash laws). Hollow chew toys (like Kongs or sterilized longbones) and a dog bed or collapsible crate are musts for housetraining. Three additional tools are required:

1. specific lures (training treats and toys) to predict and prompt specific desired behaviors;

2. rewards (praise, affection, training treats and toys) to reinforce for the dog what a lot of fun it all is; and

3. knowledge—how to convert the dog's favorite activities and games (potential distractions to training)

into "life-rewards," which may be employed to facilitate training.

The most powerful of these is knowledge. Education is the key! Watch training classes, participate in training classes, watch videos, read books, enjoy play-training with your dog and then your dog will say "Please," and your dog will say "Thank you!"

HOUSETRAINING

If dogs were left to their own devices, certainly they would chew, dig and bark for entertainment and then no doubt highlight a few areas of their living space with sprinkles of urine, in much the same way we decorate by hanging pictures. Consequently, when we ask a dog to live with us, we must teach her *where* she may dig, *where* she may perform her toilet duties, *what* she may chew and *when* she may bark. After all, when left at home alone for many hours, we cannot expect the dog to amuse herself by completing crosswords or watching the soaps on TV!

Also, it would be decidedly unfair to keep the house rules a secret from the dog, and then get angry and punish the poor critter for inevitably transgressing rules she did not even know existed. Remember: Without adequate education and guidance, the dog will be forced to establish her own rules—doggy rules—and most probably will be at odds with the owner's view of domestic living.

Since most problems develop during the first few days the dog is at home, prospective dog owners must be certain they are quite clear about the principles of housetraining *before* they get a dog. Early misbehaviors quickly become established as the *status quo*—becoming firmly entrenched as hard-to-break bad habits, which set the precedent for years to come. Make sure to teach your dog good habits right from the start. Good habits are just as hard to break as bad ones!

Ideally, when a new dog comes home, try to arrange for someone to be present as much as possible during the first few days (for adult dogs) or weeks for puppies. With only a little forethought, it is surprisingly easy to find a puppy sitter, such as a retired person, who would be willing to eat from your refrigerator and watch your television while keeping an eye on the newcomer to encourage the dog to play with chew toys and to ensure she goes outside on a regular basis.

HOUSETRAINING 1-2-3

1. Prevent Mistakes. When you can't supervise your puppy, confine her in a single room or in her crate (but don't leave her for too long!). Puppy-proof the area by laying down newspapers so that if she does make a mistake, it won't matter.

2. Teach Where. Take your puppy to the spot you want her to use every hour.

3. When she goes, praise her profusely and give her three favorite treats.

Potty Training

To teach the dog where to relieve herself:

1. never let her make a single mistake;

2. let her know where you want her to go; and

3. handsomely reward her for doing so: "GOOOOOOOD DOG!!!" liver treat, liver treat, liver treat!

Preventing Mistakes

A single mistake is a training disaster, since it heralds many more in future weeks. And each time the dog soils the house, this further reinforces the dog's unfortunate preference for an indoor, carpeted toilet. Do not let an unhousetrained dog have full run of the house.

When you are away from home, or cannot pay full attention, confine the dog to an area where elimination is appropriate, such as an outdoor run or, better still, a small, comfortable indoor kennel with access to an outdoor run. When confined in this manner, most dogs will naturally housetrain themselves.

If that's not possible, confine the dog to an area, such as a utility room, kitchen, basement or garage, where elimination may not be desired in the long run but as an interim measure it is certainly preferable to doing it all around the house. Use newspaper to cover the floor of the dog's day room. The newspaper may be used to soak up the urine and to wrap up and dispose of the feces. Once your dog develops a preferred spot for eliminating, it is only necessary to cover that part of the floor with newspaper. The smaller papered area may then be moved (only a little each day) towards the door to the outside. Thus the dog will develop the tendency to go to the door when she needs to relieve herself.

Never confine an unhousetrained dog to a crate for long periods. Doing so would force the dog to soil the crate and ruin its usefulness as an aid for housetraining (see the following discussion).

Teaching Where

In order to teach your dog where you would like her to do her business, you have to be there to direct the proceedings—an obvious, yet often neglected, fact of life. In order to be there to teach the dog where to go, you need to know *when* she needs to go. Indeed, the success of housetraining depends on the owner's ability to predict these times. Certainly, a regular feeding schedule will facilitate prediction somewhat, but there is nothing like "loading the deck" and influencing the timing of the outcome yourself!

Whenever you are at home, make sure the dog is under constant supervision and/or confined to a small area. If already well trained, simply instruct the dog to lie down in her bed or basket. Alternatively, confine the dog to a crate (doggy den) or tie-down (a short, 18-inch lead that can be clipped to an eye hook in the baseboard near her bed). Short-term close confinement strongly inhibits urination and defecation, since the dog does not want to soil her sleeping area. Thus, when you release the puppydog each hour, she will definitely need to urinate immediately and defecate every third or fourth hour. Keep the dog confined to her doggy den and take her to her intended toilet area each hour, every hour and on the hour. When taking your dog outside, instruct her to sit quietly before opening the door— she will soon learn to sit by the door when she needs to go out!

Teaching Why

Being able to predict when the dog needs to go enables the owner to be on the spot to praise and reward the dog. Each hour, hurry the dog to the intended toilet area in the yard, issue the appropriate instruction ("Go pee!" or "Go poop!"), then give the dog three to four minutes to produce. Praise and offer a couple of training treats when successful. The treats are important because many people fail to praise their dogs with feeling . . . and housetraining is hardly the time for understatement. So either loosen up and enthusiastically praise that dog: "Wuzzzer-wuzzer-wuzzer, hoooser good wuffer den? Hoooo went pee for Daddy?" Or say "Good dog!" as best you can and offer the treats for effect.

Following elimination is an ideal time for a spot of play-training in the yard or house. Also, an empty dog may be allowed greater freedom around the house for the next half hour or so, just as long as you keep an eye out to make sure she does not get into other kinds of mischief. If you are preoccupied and cannot pay full attention, confine the dog to her doggy den once more to enjoy a peaceful snooze or to play with her many chew toys.

If your dog does not eliminate within the allotted time outside—no biggie! Back to her doggy den, and then try again after another hour.

As I own large dogs, I always feel more relaxed walking an empty dog, knowing that I will not need to finish our stroll weighted down with bags of feces!

Beware of falling into the trap of walking the dog to get her to eliminate. The good ol' dog walk is such an enormous highlight in the dog's life that it represents the single biggest potential reward in domestic dogdom. However, when in a hurry, or during inclement weather, many owners abruptly terminate the walk the moment the dog has done her business.

73

This, in effect, severely punishes the dog for doing the right thing, in the right place at the right time. Consequently, many dogs become strongly inhibited from eliminating outdoors because they know it will signal an abrupt end to an otherwise thoroughly enjoyable walk.

Instead, instruct the dog to relieve herself in the yard prior to going for a walk. If you follow the above instructions, most dogs soon learn to eliminate on cue. As soon as the dog eliminates, praise (and offer a treat or two)—"Good dog! Let's go walkies!" Use the walk as a reward for eliminating in the yard. If the dog does not go, put her back in her doggy den and think about a walk later on. You will find with a "No

feces—no walk" policy, your dog will become one of the fastest defecators in the business.

If you do not have a backyard, instruct the dog to eliminate right outside your front door prior to the walk. Not only will this facilitate clean up and disposal of the feces in your own trash can but, also, the walk may again be used as a colossal reward.

CHEWING AND BARKING

Short-term close confinement also teaches the dog that occasional quiet moments are a reality of domestic living. Your puppydog is extremely impressionable during her first few weeks at home. Regular confinement

Teach your puppy that she'll be allowed to play outside after she eliminates.

at this time soon exerts a calming influence over the dog's personality. Remember, once the dog is house-trained and calmer, there will be a whole lifetime ahead for the dog to enjoy full run of the house and garden. On the other hand, by letting the newcomer have unrestricted access to the entire household and allowing her to run willy-nilly, she will most certainly develop a bunch of behavior problems in short order, no doubt necessitating confinement later in life. It would not be fair to remedially restrain and confine a dog you have trained, through neglect, to run free.

When confining the dog, make sure she always has an impressive array of suitable chew toys. Kongs and sterilized longbones (both readily available from pet stores) make the best chew toys, since they are hollow and may be stuffed with treats to heighten the dog's interest. For example, by stuffing the little hole at the top of a Kong with a small piece of freeze-dried liver, the dog will not want to leave it alone.

Remember, treats do not have to be junk food and they certainly should not represent extra calories. Rather, treats should be part of each dog's regular daily diet: Some food

may be served in the dog's bowl for breakfast and dinner, some food may be used as training treats, and some food may be used for stuffing chew toys. I regularly stuff my dogs' many Kongs with different shaped biscuits and kibble. The kibble seems to fall out fairly easily, as do the oval-shaped biscuits, thus rewarding the dog instantaneously for checking out the chew toys. The bone-shaped biscuits fall out after a while, rewarding the dog for worrying at the chew toy. But the triangular biscuits never come out. They remain inside the Kong as lures, maintaining the dog's fascination with her chew toy. To further focus the dog's interest, I always make sure to flavor the triangular biscuits by rubbing them with a little cheese or freeze-dried liver.

If stuffed chew toys are reserved especially for times the dog is confined, the puppydog will soon learn to enjoy quiet moments in her doggy den and she will quickly develop a chew-toy habit—a good habit! This is a simple autoshaping process; all the owner has to do is set up the situation and the dog all but trains herself—easy and effective. Even when the dog is given run of the house, her first inclination will be to indulge her rewarding chew-toy habit

playing with her chew toys when she expects you to return. Since most owner-absent misbehavior happens right after you leave and right before your expected return, your puppydog will now be conveniently preoccupied with her chew toys at these times.

COME AND SIT

Most puppies will happily approach virtually anyone, whether called or not; that is, until they collide with adolescence and develop other more important doggy interests, such as sniffing a multiplicity of exquisite odors on the grass. Your mission, Mr./Ms. Owner, is to teach and reward the pup for coming reliably, willingly and happily when called—and you have just three months to get it done. Unless adequately reinforced, your puppy's tendency to approach people will self-destruct by adolescence.

Call your dog ("Fido, come!"), open your arms (and maybe squat down) as a welcoming signal, waggle a treat or toy as a lure and reward the puppydog when she comes running. Do not wait to praise the dog until she reaches you—she may come 95 percent of the way and then run off after some distraction. Instead, praise the dog's first step towards you and

No matter what you are training your Cocker Spaniel to do, remember to praise her profusely for a job well done.

rather than destroy less-attractive household articles, such as curtains, carpets, chairs and compact disks. Similarly, a chew-toy chewer will be less inclined to scratch and chew herself excessively. Also, if the dog busies herself as a recreational chewer, she will be less inclined to develop into a recreational barker or digger when left at home alone.

Stuff a number of chew toys whenever the dog is left confined and remove the extra-special-tasting treats when you return. Your dog will now amuse herself with her chew toys before falling asleep and then resume continue praising enthusiastically for every step she takes in your direction.

When the rapidly approaching puppy dog is three lengths away from impact, instruct her to sit ("Fido, sit!") and hold the lure in front of you in an outstretched hand to prevent her from hitting you mid-chest and knocking you flat on your back! As Fido decelerates to nose the lure, move the treat upwards and backwards just over her muzzle with an upwards motion of your extended arm (palm-upwards). As the dog looks up to follow the lure, she will sit down (if she jumps up, you are holding the lure too high). Praise the dog for sitting. Move backwards and call her again. Repeat this many times over, always praising when Fido comes and sits; on occasion, reward her.

For the first couple of trials, use a training treat both as a lure to entice the dog to come and sit and as a reward for doing so. Thereafter, try to use different items as lures and rewards. For example, lure the dog with a Kong or Frisbee but reward her with a food treat. Or lure the dog with a food treat but pat her and throw a tennis ball as a reward. After just a few repetitions, dispense with the lures and rewards; the dog will begin to respond willingly to your verbal requests and hand signals just for the prospect of praise from your heart and affection from your hands.

Instruct every family member, friend and visitor how to get the dog to come and sit. Invite people over for a series of pooch parties; do not keep the pup a secret—let other people enjoy this puppy, and let the pup enjoy other people. Puppydog parties are not only fun, they easily attract a lot of people to help you train your dog. Unless you teach your dog how to meet people, that is, to sit for greetings, no doubt the dog will resort to jumping up. Then you and the visitors will get annoyed, and the dog will be punished. This is not fair. Send out those invitations for puppy parties and teach your dog to be mannerly and socially acceptable.

Even though your dog quickly masters obedient recalls in the house, her reliability may falter when playing in the backyard or local park. Ironically, it is the owner who has unintentionally trained the dog not to respond in these instances. By allowing the dog to play and run around and otherwise have a good time, but then to call the dog to put her on leash to take her home, the dog quickly learns playing is fun but training is a drag. Thus, playing in the park becomes a severe distraction, which works against training. Bad news!

Instead, whether playing with the dog off leash or on leash, request her to come at frequent intervals—say, every minute or so. On most occasions, praise and pet the dog for a few seconds while she is sitting, then tell her to go play again. For especially fast recalls, offer a couple of training treats and take the time to praise and pet the dog enthusiastically before releasing her. The dog will learn that coming when called is not necessarily the end of the play session, and neither is it the end of the world; rather, it signals an enjoyable, quality time-out with the owner before resuming play once more. In fact, playing in the park now becomes a very effective life-reward, which works to facilitate training by reinforcing each obedient and timely recall. Good news!

SIT, DOWN, STAND AND ROLLOVER

Teaching the dog a variety of body positions is easy for owner and dog, impressive for spectators and extremely useful for all. Using lure-reward techniques, it is possible to train several positions at once to verbal commands or hand signals (which impress the socks off onlookers).

Sit and down—the two control commands—prevent or resolve nearly a hundred behavior problems. For example, if the dog happily and obediently sits or lies down when requested, she cannot jump on visitors, dash out the front door, run around and chase her tail, pester other dogs, harass cats or annoy family, friends or strangers. Additionally, "Sit" or "Down" are the best emergency commands for off-leash control.

It is easier to teach and maintain a reliable sit than maintain a reliable recall. Sit is the purest and simplest of commands—either the dog is sitting or she is not. If there is any change of circumstances or potential danger in the park, for example, simply instruct the dog to sit. If she sits, you have a number of options: Allow the dog to resume playing when she is safe, walk up and put the dog on leash or call the dog. The dog will be much more likely to come when called if she has already acknowledged her compliance by sitting. If the dog does not sit in the park—train her to!

Stand and rollover-stay are the two positions for examining the dog.

Your veterinarian will love you to distraction if you take a little time to teach the dog to stand still and roll over and play possum. Also, your vet bills will be smaller because it will take the veterinarian less time to examine your dog. The rollover-stay is an especially useful command and is really just a variation of the down-stay: Whereas the dog lies prone in the traditional down, she lies supine in the rollover-stay.

As with teaching come and sit, the training techniques to teach the dog to assume all other body positions on cue are user-friendly and dog-friendly. Simply give the appropriate request, lure the dog into the desired body position using a training treat or toy and then praise (and maybe reward) the dog as soon as she complies. Try not to touch the dog to get her to respond. If you teach the dog by guiding her into position, the dog will quickly learn that rump-pressure means sit, for example, but as yet you still have no control over your dog if she is just 6 feet away. It will still be necessary to teach the dog to sit on request. So do not make training a time-consuming two-step process; instead, teach the dog to sit to a verbal request or hand signal from the outset. Once the dog sits willingly when

requested, by all means use your hands to pet the dog when she does so.

To teach down when the dog is already sitting, say "Fido, down!," hold the lure in one hand (palm down) and lower that hand to the floor between the dog's forepaws. As the dog lowers her head to follow the lure, slowly move the lure away from the dog just a fraction (in front of her paws). The dog will lie down as she stretches her nose forward to follow the lure. Praise the dog when she does so. If the dog stands up, you pulled the lure away too far and too quickly.

When teaching the dog to lie down from the standing position, say "Down" and lower the lure to the floor as before. Once the dog has lowered her forequarters and assumed a play bow, gently and slowly move the lure towards the dog between her forelegs. Praise the dog as soon as her rear end plops down.

After just a couple of trials it will be possible to alternate sits and downs and have the dog energetically perform doggy push-ups. Praise the dog a lot, and after half a dozen or so push-ups reward the dog with a training treat or toy. You will notice the more energetically you move your arm—upwards (palm up) to get the dog to sit, and downwards (palm

79

down) to get the dog to lie down—the more energetically the dog responds to your requests. Now try training the dog in silence and you will notice she has also learned to respond to hand signals. Yeah! Not too shabby for the first session.

To teach stand from the sitting position, say "Fido, stand," slowly move the lure half a dog-length away from the dog's nose, keeping it at nose level, and praise the dog as she stands to follow the lure. As soon as the dog stands, lower the lure to just beneath the dog's chin to entice her to look down; otherwise she will stand and then sit immediately. To prompt the dog to stand from the down position, move the lure half a dog-length upwards and away from the dog, holding the lure at standing nose height from the floor.

Teaching rollover is best started from the down position, with the dog lying on one side, or at least with both hind legs stretched out on the same side. Say "Fido, bang!" and move the lure backwards and alongside the dog's muzzle to her elbow (on the side of her outstretched hind legs). Once the dog looks to the side and backwards, very slowly move the lure upwards to the dog's shoulder and backbone. Tickling the dog in the

goolies (groin area) often invokes a reflex-raising of the hind leg as an appeasement gesture, which facilitates the tendency to roll over. If you move the lure too quickly and the dog jumps into the standing position, have patience and start again. As soon as the dog rolls onto her back, keep the lure stationary and mesmerize the dog with a relaxing tummy rub.

To teach rollover-stay when the dog is standing or moving, say "Fido, bang!" and give the appropriate hand signal (with index finger pointed and thumb cocked in true Sam Spade fashion), then in one fluid movement lure her to first lie down and then rollover-stay as above.

Teaching the dog to stay in each of the above four positions becomes a piece of cake after first teaching the dog not to worry at the toy or treat training lure. This is best accomplished by hand feeding dinner kibble. Hold a piece of kibble firmly in your hand and softly instruct "Off!" Ignore any licking and slobbering for however long the dog worries at the treat, but say "Take it!" and offer the kibble *the instant* the dog breaks contact with her muzzle. Repeat this a few times, and then up the ante and insist the dog remove her muzzle for one whole second before offering the kibble. Then progressively refine your criteria and have the dog not touch your hand (or treat) for longer and longer periods on each trial, such as for two seconds, four seconds, then six, ten, fifteen, twenty, thirty seconds and so on.

The dog soon learns: (1) worrying at the treat never gets results, whereas (2) noncontact is often rewarded after a variable time lapse.

Teaching "Off!" has many useful applications in its own right. Additionally, instructing the dog not to touch a training lure often produces spontaneous and magical stays. Request the dog to stand-stay, for example, and not to touch the lure. At first set your sights on a short two-second stay before rewarding the dog. (Remember, every long journey begins with a single step.) However, on subsequent trials, gradually and progressively increase the length of stay required to receive a reward. In no time at all your dog will stand calmly for a minute or so.

RELEVANCY TRAINING

Once you have taught the dog what you expect her to do when requested to come, sit, lie down, stand, rollover and stay, the time is right to teach the dog why she should comply with your wishes. The secret is to have many (many) extremely short training interludes (two to five seconds each) at numerous (numerous) times during the course of the dog's day. Especially work with the dog immediately before the dog's good times and during the dog's good times. For example, ask your dog to sit and/or

This well-trained Cocker Spaniel enjoys a walk with her owner.

lie down each time before opening doors, serving meals, offering treats and tummy rubs; ask the dog to perform a few controlled doggy push-ups before letting her off leash or throwing a tennis ball; and perhaps request the dog to sit-down-sit-stand-down-stand-rollover before inviting her to cuddle on the couch.

Similarly, request the dog to sit many times during play or on walks, and in no time at all the dog will be only too pleased to follow your instructions because she has learned that a compliant response heralds all sorts of goodies. Basically all you are trying to teach the dog is how to say please: "Please throw the tennis ball. Please may I snuggle on the couch."

Remember, it is important to keep training interludes short and to have many short sessions each and every day. The shortest (and most useful) session comprises asking the dog to sit and then go play during a play session. When trained this way, your dog will soon associate training with good times. In fact, the dog may be unable to distinguish between training and good times and, indeed, there should be no distinction. The warped concept that training involves forcing the dog to comply and/or dominating her will

is totally at odds with the picture of a truly well-trained dog. In reality, enjoying a game of training with a dog is no different from enjoying a game of backgammon or tennis with a friend; and walking with a dog should be no different from strolling with a spouse, or with buddies on the golf course.

WALK BY YOUR SIDE

Many people attempt to teach a dog to heel by putting her on a leash and physically correcting the dog when she makes mistakes. There are a number of things seriously wrong with this approach, the first being that most people do not want precision heeling; rather, they simply want the dog to follow or walk by their side. Second, when physically restrained during "training," even though the dog may grudgingly mope by your side when "handcuffed" on leash, let's see what happens when she is off leash. History! The dog is in the next county because she never enjoyed walking with you on leash and you have no control over her off leash. So let's just teach the dog off leash from the outset to want to walk with us. Third, if the dog has not been trained to heel, it is a trifle hasty to think about punishing the poor dog for making mistakes and breaking heeling rules she didn't even know existed. This is simply not fair! Surely, if the dog had been adequately taught how to heel, she would seldom make mistakes and hence there would be no need to correct the dog. Remember, each mistake and each correction (punishment) advertise the trainer's inadequacy, not the dog's. The dog is not stubborn, she is not stupid and she is not bad. Even if she were, she would still require training, so let's train her properly.

Let's teach the dog to enjoy following us and to want to walk by our side off leash. Then it will be easier to teach high-precision off-leash heeling patterns if desired. Before going on outdoor walks, it is necessary to teach the dog not to pull. Then it becomes easy to teach on-leash walking and heeling because the dog already wants to walk with you, she is familiar with the desired walking and heeling positions and she knows not to pull.

83

FOLLOWING

Start by training your dog to follow you. Many puppies will follow if you simply walk away from them and maybe click your fingers or chuckle. Adult dogs may require additional enticement to stimulate them to follow, such as a training lure or, at the very least, a lively trainer. To teach the dog to follow: (1) keep walking and (2) walk away from the dog. If the dog attempts to lead or lag, change pace; slow down if the dog forges too far ahead, but speed up if

If your puppy starts pulling or biting on the leash, stand still and wait for her to stop.

This well-trained Cocker Spaniel heels off-lead with precision.

park to do this. Indoors, entice the dog to follow upstairs, into a bedroom, into the bathroom, downstairs, around the living room couch, zigzagging between dining room chairs and into the kitchen for dinner. Outdoors, get the dog to follow around park benches, trees, shrubs and along walkways and lines in the grass. (For safety outdoors, it is advisable to attach a long line on the dog, but never exert corrective tension on the line.)

Remember, following has a lot to do with attitude—your attitude! Most probably your dog will not want to follow Mr. Grumpy Troll with the personality of wilted lettuce. Lighten up—walk with a jaunty step, whistle a happy tune, sing, skip and tell jokes to your dog and she will be right there by your side.

she lags too far behind. Say "Steady!" or "Easy!" each time before you slow down and "Quickly!" or "Hustle!" each time before you speed up, and the dog will learn to change pace on cue. If the dog lags or leads too far, or if she wanders right or left, simply walk quickly in the opposite direction and maybe even run away from the dog and hide.

Practicing is a lot of fun; you can set up a course in your home, yard or

THE IMPORTANCE OF TRICKS

Nothing will improve a dog's quality of life better than having a few tricks under her belt. Teaching any trick expands the dog's vocabulary, which facilitates communication and improves the owner's control. Also, specific tricks help prevent and resolve specific behavior problems.

For example, by teaching the dog to fetch her toys, the dog learns carrying a toy makes the owner happy and, therefore, will be more likely to chew her toy than other inappropriate items.

Tricks facilitate training. For example, by the time the owner has enjoyed teaching her dog the "ol' balance the biscuit on the nose" trick, she already has a dynamite sit-stay!

More important, teaching tricks prompts owners to lighten up and train with a sunny disposition. Really, tricks should be no different from any other behaviors we put on cue. But they are. When teaching tricks, owners have a much sweeter attitude, which in turn motivates the dog and improves her willingness to comply. The dog feels tricks are a blast, but formal commands are a drag. In fact, tricks are so enjoyable, they may be used as rewards in training by asking the dog to come, sit and down-stay and then rollover for a tummy rub. Go on, try it: Crack a smile and even giggle when the dog promptly and willingly lies down and stays.

Most important, performing tricks prompts onlookers to smile and giggle. Many people are scared of dogs, especially large ones. And nothing can be more off-putting for a dog

TOYS THAT EARN THEIR KEEP

To entertain even the most distracted of dogs, while you're home or away, have a selection of the following toys on hand: hollow chew toys (like Kongs, sterilized hollow longbones and cubes or balls that can be stuffed with kibble). Smear peanut butter or honey on the inside of the hollow toy or bone and stuff the bone with kibble and your dog will think of nothing else but working the object to get at the food. Great to take your dog's mind off the fact that you've left the house.

than to be constantly confronted by strangers who don't like her because of her size or the way she looks. Uneasy people put the dog on edge, causing her to back off and bark, only frightening people all the more. And so a vicious circle develops, with the people's fear fueling the dog's fear *and vice versa*. Instead, tie a pink ribbon to your dog's collar and practice all sorts of tricks on walks and in the park, and you will be pleasantly amazed how it changes people's attitudes toward your friendly dog.

The dog's repertoire of tricks is limited only by the trainer's imagination. Below I have described three of my favorites:

85

Speak and Shush

The training sequence involved in teaching a dog to bark on request is no different from that used when training any behavior on cue: request—lure—response—reward. As always, the secret of success lies in finding an effective lure. If the dog always barks at the doorbell, for example, say "Rover, speak!", have an accomplice ring the doorbell, then reward the dog for barking. After a few woofs, ask Rover to "Shush!", waggle a food treat under her nose (to entice her to sniff and thus to shush), praise her when quiet and eventually offer the treat as a reward. Alternate "Speak" and "Shush," progressively increasing the length of shush-time between each barking bout.

Play Bow

With the dog standing, say "Bow!" and lower the food lure (palm upwards) to rest between the dog's forepaws. Praise as the dog lowers her forequarters and sternum to the ground (as when teaching the down),

but then lure the dog to stand and offer the treat. On successive trials, gradually increase the length of time the dog is required to remain in the play bow posture in order to gain a food reward. If the dog's rear end collapses into a down, say nothing and offer no reward; simply start over.

Be a Bear

With the dog sitting backed into a corner to prevent her from toppling over backwards, say "Be a bear!" With bent paw and palm down, raise a lure upwards and backwards along the top of the dog's muzzle. Praise the dog when she sits up on her haunches and offer the treat as a reward. To prevent the dog from standing on her hind legs, keep the lure closer to the dog's muzzle. On each trial, progressively increase the length of time the dog is required to sit up to receive a food reward. Since lure-reward training is so easy, teach the dog to stand and walk on her hind legs as well!

Resources

BOOKS

About Cocker Spaniels

Austin, Norman A., and Jean S. Austin. *The Complete American Cocker Spaniel.* New York: Howell Book House, 1993.

Grosman, Alvin. *The American Cocker Spaniel: The Pure Breeds.* Wilsonville, OR: Doral Publishing, 1990.

About Health Care

American Kennel Club. *American Kennel Club Dog Care and Training.* New York: Howell Book House, 1991.

Carlson, Delbert, DVM, and James Giffin, MD. *Dog Owner's Home Veterinary Handbook.* New York: Howell Book House, 1992.

DeBitetto, James, DVM, and Sarah Hodgson. *You & Your Puppy.* New York: Howell Book House, 1995.

Lane, Marion. *The Humane Society of the United States Complete Guide to Dog Care.* New York: Little, Brown & Co., 1998.

Schwartz, Stephanie, DVM. *First Aid for Dogs: An Owner's Guide to a Happy Healthy Pet.* New York: Howell Book House, 1998.

Volhard, Wendy and Kerry L. Brown. *The Holistic Guide for a Healthy Dog.* New York: Howell Book House, 1995.

About Training

Arden, Andrea. *Train Your Dog The Lazy Way.* New York: Howell Book House, 1998.

Benjamin, Carol Lea. *Mother Knows Best.* New York: Howell Book House, 1985.

Bohnenkamp, Gwen. *Manners for the Modern Dog.* San Francisco: Perfect Paws, 1990.

Dog Behavior: An Owner's Guide to a Happy Healthy Pet. New York: Howell Book House, 1998.

Dunbar, Ian, Ph.D., MRCVS. *Dr. Dunbar's Good Little Book.* James & Kenneth Publishers, 2140 Shattuck Ave. #2406, Berkeley, CA 94704. (510) 658-8588. Order from Publisher.

Evans, Job Michael. *People, Pooches and Problems.* New York: Howell Book House, 1991.

Foster, Race, DVM and Marty Smith. *Right from the Start*. New York: Howell Book House, 1998.

Palika, Liz. *All Dogs Need Some Training*. New York: Howell Book House, 1997.

Volhard, Jack and Melissa Bartlett. *What All Good Dogs Should Know: The Sensible Way to Train*. New York: Howell Book House, 1991.

About Activities

Hall, Lynn. *Dog Showing for Beginners*. New York: Howell Book House, 1994.

O'Neil, Jackie. *All About Agility*. New York: Howell Book House, 1998.

Simmons-Moake, Jane. *Agility Training, The Fun Sport for All Dogs*. New York: Howell Book House, 1991.

Vanacore, Connie. *Dog Showing: An Owner's Guide*. New York: Howell Book House, 1990.

Volhard, Jack and Wendy. *The Canine Good Citizen*. New York: Howell Book House, 1994.

MAGAZINES

The AKC GAZETTE, The Official Journal for the Sport of Purebred Dogs
American Kennel Club
260 Madison Ave.
New York, NY 10014
www.akc.org

DOG & KENNEL
7-L Dundas Circle
Greensboro, NC 27407
(336) 292-4047
www.dogandkennel.com

DOG FANCY
Fancy Publications
3 Burroughs
Irvine, CA 92618
(714) 855-8822
http://dogfancy.com

DOG WORLD
Maclean Hunter Publishing Corp.
500 N. Dearborn, Ste. 1100
Chicago, IL 60610
(312) 396-0600
www.dogworldmag.com

PETLIFE: YOUR COMPANION ANIMAL MAGAZINE
Magnolia Media Group
1400 Two Tandy Center
Fort Worth, TX 76102
(800) 767-9377
www.petlifeweb.com

MORE INFORMATION ABOUT COCKER SPANIELS

National Breed Club

AMERICAN SPANIEL CLUB
Corresponding Secretary:
    Ellen Passage
    35 Academy Road
    Hohokus, NJ 07423
Breeder Contact:
    Dorothy Mustard
    30 Cardinal Loop
    Crossville, TN 38555
Breed Rescue:
    Becki Zaborowski
    (770) 974-7931

The Club can send you information on all aspects of the breed including the names and addresses of breed clubs in your area, as well as obedience clubs. Inquire about membership.

The American Kennel Club

The American Kennel Club (AKC), devoted to the advancement of purebred dogs, is the oldest and largest registry organization in this country. Every breed recognized by the AKC has a national (parent) club. National clubs are a great source of information on your breed. The affiliated clubs hold AKC events and use AKC rules to hold performance events, dog shows, educational programs, health clinics and training classes. The AKC staff is divided between offices in New York City and Raleigh, North Carolina. The AKC has an excellent Web site that provides information on the organization and all AKC-recognized breeds. The address is **www.akc.org.**

For registration and performance events information, or for customer service, contact:

THE AMERICAN KENNEL CLUB
5580 Centerview Dr., Suite 200
Raleigh, NC 27606
(919) 233-9767

The AKC's executive offices and the AKC Library (open to the public) are at this address:

THE AMERICAN KENNEL CLUB
260 Madison Ave.
New York, New York 10016
(212) 696-8200 (general information)
(212) 696-8246 (AKC Library)
www.akc.org

UNITED KENNEL CLUB
100 E. Kilgore Rd.
Kalamazoo, MI 49001-5598
(616) 343-9020
www.ukcdogs.com

AMERICAN RARE BREED ASSOCIATION
9921 Frank Tippett Rd.
Cheltenham, MD 20623
(301) 868-5718 (voice or fax)
www.arba.org

CANADIAN KENNEL CLUB
89 Skyway Ave., Ste. 100
Etobicoke, Ontario
Canada M9W 6R4
(416) 675-5511
www.ckc.ca

ORTHOPEDIC FOUNDATION FOR ANIMALS (OFA)
2300 E. Nifong Blvd.
Columbia, MO 65201-3856
(314) 442-0418
www.offa.org

Trainers

Animal Behavior & Training Associates (ABTA)
9018 Balboa Blvd., Ste. 591
Northridge, CA 91325
(800) 795-3294
www.Good-dawg.com

Association of Pet Dog Trainers (APDT)
(800) PET-DOGS
www.apdt.com

National Association of Dog Obedience Instructors (NADOI)
729 Grapevine Highway, Ste. 369
Hurst, TX 76054-2085
www.kimberly.uidaho.edu/nadoi

Associations

Delta Society
P.O. Box 1080
Renton, WA 98507-1080
(Promotes the human/animal bond
through pet-assisted therapy and other
programs)
www.petsform.com/DELTASOCIETY/
dsi400.htm

Dog Writers Association of America
(DWAA)
Sally Cooper, Secretary
222 Woodchuck Lane
Harwinton, CT 06791
www.dwaa.org

National Association for Search and
Rescue (NASAR)
4500 Southgate Place, Ste. 100
Chantilly, VA 20157
(703) 222-6277
www.nasar.org

Therapy Dogs International
6 Hilltop Rd.
Mendham, NJ 07945

OTHER USEFUL RESOURCES— WEB SITES

General Information— Links to Additional Sites, On-Line Shopping

www.acmepet.com – a fun site for pet
lovers

www.k9web.com – resources for the dog
world

www.netpet.com – pet related products,
software and services

www.apapets.com – The American Pet
Association

www.dogandcatbooks.com – book
catalog

www.dogbooks.com – on-line bookshop

www.baddogs.com – for when your
pooch has gotten into trouble

www.animal.discovery.com/ – cable
television channel on-line

Health

www.avma.org – American Veterinary
Medical Association (AVMA)

www.avma.org/care4pets/avmaloss.htm –
AVMA site dedicated to consideration of euthanizing sick pets and the
grieving process after losing a pet.

www.aplb.org – Association for Pet Loss
Bereavement (APLB)—contains an
index of national hot lines for on-line
and office counseling.

www.netfopets.com/AskTheExperts.
html – veterinary questions answered
on-line.

Breed Information

www.bestdogs.com/news/ – newsgroup

www.cheta.net/connect/canine/breeds/ –
Canine Connections Breed Information
Index